OUTRAGEOUS LOVE

He Never Turned Away

**A Memoir of Healing &
an Invitation into the Father's Embrace**

by

LAWRENCE PRASAD

An inner healing minister and companion
to leaders and the wounded.

OUTRAGEOUS LOVE

He Never Turned Away

Copyright © 2026 by **Lawrence Prasad**

Scripture quotations are taken from:

The Passion Translation (TPT), copyright © 2017, 2018, 2020 by Passion & Fire Ministries, Inc. All rights reserved.

The Message (MSG), copyright © 1993, 2002, 2018 by Eugene H. Peterson. All rights reserved.

The Mirror Bible, copyright © by François du Toit.

The Remedy Bible, copyright © by Timothy R. Jennings, MD.

New Living Translation (NLT), copyright © 1996, 2004, 2015 by Tyndale House Foundation.

Published by: Heart Keys
ISBN: 978-1-7645370-0-1 (Print)
ISBN: 978-1-7645370-1-8 (eBook)
ISBN: 978-1-7645370-2-5 (Audiobook)

Cover design by: Lawrence Prasad and Jacob Rivera
Interior design by: Lawrence Prasad and Amit Dey

Printed in: United States of America
First Edition: March 2026

For more information:
Website: www.lawrenceprasad.com
Email: info@lawrenceprasad.com

Content Warning: This book contains descriptions of childhood trauma, sexual abuse, substance use, and complex family dynamics. Reader discretion is advised. If you are a survivor of trauma, please proceed with care and consider reading with a trusted friend, counsellor, or support person nearby.

Disclaimer: This book is written in Australian English.

TABLE OF CONTENTS

DEDICATION

To my mum, Pearl, and my Aunty Wendy, my greatest intercessors, my first teachers of prayer, my examples of faithful love. Thank you for never giving up on me, for praying me through the darkest seasons, and for introducing me to the Holy Spirit. You are heroes of the faith, and I honour you both.

To (Aussie) John and Pauline Arnott thank you for loving me unconditionally for those significant twelve years. Thank you for never bringing correction that caused separation, never withdrawing love, never giving up. You showed me what the Father's love looks like in human form. I am forever grateful.

To John and Carol Arnott and the Catch the Fire family thank you for creating a space where the Father's love is tangible, where encounter is normal, where healing flows freely. **International Leaders School of Ministry** changed my life. You changed my life.

To Peter Sharp thank you for being a father to me when I didn't have one present. Thank you for stepping in, for loving me, for putting boundaries in place, for showing me what a good father looks like. You made a difference in my life that I can never repay.

To Jordan, Grace, and Amelia being your uncle and getting to father you has been one of the greatest joys of my life. I pray you always know whose you are, that you walk in your identity as beloved children of the Father, and that you break every chain that tried to hold our family captive. I love you.

To the Father, Jesus, and Holy Spirit, You are the reason for everything. Thank You for Your outrageous love. Thank You for never giving up on me. Thank You for healing me, restoring me, and using my story to bring freedom to others. I am Yours, forever, never separated. Oneness.

ACKNOWLEDGEMENTS

This book would not exist without the countless people who have walked with me, loved me, and believed in me, even when I didn't believe in myself.

To Dubb Alexander: thank you for your friendship, and for the many conversations that helped me see the Father's heart more clearly through Jesus. Your encouragement has shaped my life and ministry in profound ways.

To Connie Sinnott: Thank you for teaching me how to receive. That hug, that moment, that six-month assignment — it changed everything. You are a spiritual mother, and I honour you.

To Diane Pearce: Thank you for speaking life, restoration, healing, and destiny over me and into my being in 1999. That 25-minute prophetic encounter reached parts of me that had never had a voice. You were a catalyst for transformation.

To Annie Layton: You have worn many hats in my life — pastor, pastoral supervisor, mentor, but the greatest gift you've given me is friendship. Thank you for seeing me, for holding space for my mess, for never flinching when I brought you the hard stuff. Thank you for walking with me through the valleys and celebrating with me on the mountaintops. You've taught me what it means to be truly known and deeply loved. I'm grateful beyond words.

To Travis: Thank you for being the friend who invited me to invite Jesus into my mess. That simple invitation changed the trajectory of my life.

To my Heart Keys Intercessors: Thank you for holding me in constant prayer, and allowing me to be effective in the ministry God has called me into. Your prayer and prophetic consultation always bless the many we get to love back to life.

To my sister Madeleine: You have taught me more than you know. Watching you live with such joy, grace, and courage in the face of your dual disability has shown me what true strength looks like. You remind me every day that joy is not the absence of hardship, but the presence of love. You are a gift, and I honour you, my sister.

To my sister Annabel, and to Malakhy, Asth'ella, Evangeline, and Trinity: Thank you for being part of this journey and for letting me be part of yours. I pray you always know how deeply loved you are, and that you walk in the freedom and identity the Father has for you. I love you all.

To my brother Raj: you are my brother, and I honour the bond we share. I release you into the Father's hands. May we both find the freedom and peace we're searching for. I love you.

To my dad, Hari: Thank you for doing your best with what you had. I honour you, I forgive you, and I release you. The cycle stops here. I love you dad.

To the Heart Keys and Professional Pastoral Partnership communities: Thank you for trusting me with your stories, your wounds, and your hearts. It is the greatest privilege of my life to walk with you on the journey of healing, transformation and restoration.

ENDORSEMENTS

I have known Lawrence Prasad for approximately 25 years, and I have found him to be a very faithful and sincere lover of Jesus.

His book reminds us how incredibly patient and kind our heavenly Father truly is. His arms are open for us continuously as we wrestle through the transformation of His refining work in us. We are reminded that we are all broken people, we have all fallen short of the Glory of God. But He promises to complete the work He has begun in us until the day of Jesus Christ. We are called to walk it out with each-other as the Lord transforms us, so that we can become all that our Heavenly Father intends for us to be; patient, kind, full of His Spirit with open arms to embrace each other in our moments of brokenness.

Thank you, Lawrence, for your vulnerability and willingness to share your testimony. May this book bring freedom to many and a new revelation of how deep our Father's love is for each one of us.

John Arnott - Founder Catch the Fire World –
Formerly Toronto Airport Christian Fellowship
(Known Globally as the Father's Blessing / Toronto Blessing)

"Outrageous Love is a beautiful, courageous invitation back into the loving embrace of God, our true Father, through Jesus Christ. Lawrence Prasad writes with incredible vulnerability, honesty, and deep compassion. Sharing his profound journey from extreme brokenness to freedom and wholeness, Lawrence brilliantly creates a safe space where we can encounter the presence and power of the Holy Spirit without religious pressure or pretence. This book will draw you in with extraordinary stories while inviting you to engage in powerful tools and practical exercises that, together with the Holy Spirit, have the potential to set you free from trauma, shame, and striving and restore you to knowing what it truly means to be accepted as a beloved son or daughter in God's love. You will learn from Lawrence what it means to be an overcomer, walking in powerful divine favor, blessing, and honor.

We joyfully recommend this amazing book."

Duncan & Kate Smith - *Presidents,*
Catch The Fire World

"Wow! This is one of the best books I've read in a long time. I first met Lawrence in Fiji when we were both part of a team leading the same **International Leaders School of Ministry**, where Lawrence had his encounter years earlier in Melbourne. No one misses Lawrence when he enters a room. He's bigger than life, and fills the space with his personality. Several years later I met him at **Catch The Fire Melbourne**, pastored by two of his spiritual parents and mentors, John and Pauline Arnott. In those years, he had changed. He's matured as a follower of Jesus, and he's grown in his ability to impart the transformation he had received (and was still receiving). This book is about discovering who you are by discovering that God's love will find you. Lawrence is a captivating writer; you will be drawn into his story, his journey, and his discoveries. And the practical help Lawrence gives at the end of each chapter will — hear me say it — bring Father God's outrageous love into your life!"

Steve Long - *Former Senior Leader of* **Catch the Fire Toronto***, Vice President –* **Catch The Fire World***, Sphere Leader - Europe, Middle East, and Africa*

"I love Lawrence Prasad and *Outrageous Love*. It reads like an extension of who he is — honest, brave, tender, and relentlessly anchored in the goodness of God. There is healing in this book. The reader is invited into a slow, sacred re-storying where shame loses its voice, and love gets the final word. Lawrence writes with the kind of clarity that only comes from having walked the long road home. When he writes, "He didn't transform me through condemnation… He transformed me through love," you can feel the weight of lived truth behind every word and an invitation. In the pages of this book, you'll discover Jesus is walking with you, reminding you again and again that the Father has always been closer than you dared to hope, and that, in Lawrence's words, "He never turned away." And He never will."

Jason Clark - *Author of "Leaving and Finding Jesus" and host of "Rethinking God with Tacos" www.afamilystory.org*

"Many excellent teachings are available for us from different streams — prophecy, discipleship, faith, hope, and more. But they all need to rest on the bookshelf that is called the Father's Love. In Lawrence's book, he details in great depth his challenges, but more importantly, his victory in the arms of his heavenly Father. His book is very personal, and he shows great courage in sharing his walk with the drag/nightclub scene. He demonstrates a wonderful, positive, loving response to those in the LGBTQ family. His story is a journal of invitation — not only through his testimonies but through practical exercises in the 'Heart Work' sections at the end of each chapter. This book will draw you into the 'how' and 'why' of the heart of our Father.

We are sure it will be incredibly helpful to those who are presently struggling through the same issues, to show how the Father's love can take them to victory. We are so proud of him as a spiritual son and are so happy we have been able to be a small part of his journey."

Jeremy & Connie Sinnott - *Senior Pastors* – ***Catch the Fire Barrie***, *Founding Worship Leaders*, ***Catch The Fire Toronto***, *International Trainers with* ***Catch The Fire***

"A man asked Jesus 'What must I do to inherit eternal life?' (Mark 10:17-22)

This is THE question we all ask at some time – though it's more likely to be something like 'how do I have a relationship with God?' This splendid book provides the answers we are seeking and I wholeheartedly recommend it to all seekers. Lawrence introduces it as 'A Memoir of Healing & an Invitation into the Father's Embrace'. He writes frankly and openly about his journey seeking God – the many temptations, traumas and mixed messages he endures as well as the insights, healings and new beginnings. At every point we enter into his searching and longing and his gradual insight into the love of God for him. He shares his moments of breakthrough, new insight, letting go, embracing transformation, and he confidently steps into a new way of being himself and being available to accompany others in their seeking. He shows how God steps into our darkest memories, restores our identity and never turns away.

Most helpfully, each Part concludes with Heart Work Invitations, suggestions for reflection, prayer and encounter. He says 'These aren't just questions to answer; they're invitations to engage with the Father, to let Jesus into your story, and to experience the Holy Spirit's comfort and guidance.'

If you are a person haunted by memories of the past, by decisions you now regret, or by a longing for God that never seems to get anywhere — or perhaps you go through life in your own way and strength and never give a thought to God, whoever or whatever that means — I am sure that, if you are a person living and breathing, you will find life, wisdom, and direction in reading this book. Above all, you will encounter love, acceptance, belonging, healing, and purpose for moving forward. You will encounter and be embraced by Outrageous Love."

John W Stewart - *ThL (ACT), MMin (MCD), Anglican priest, Life Member of Australian Network Spiritual Direction, spiritual director and pastoral supervisor.*

"I have had the privilege of being friends with Lawrence for many years. Outrageous Love is not only the title of his book — it is a defining characteristic of his life. When his name is mentioned, it is often followed by comments about the genuine love that flows so naturally from him. Lawrence writes with humility and transparency, inviting readers into his own personal transformation through encountering the love of our Heavenly Father. This book serves as a practical guide, leading us deeper into a revelation of the Father's love and into authentic heart healing. The tools and testimonies within these pages will stir readers toward a deeper walk with God, whether they are new believers or seasoned leaders in the Body of Christ.

I highly recommend you grab a copy and begin the journey."

Wendy Hayes - *MComCouns, Counsellor, Co-Founder*
Australian Inner Healing Network, ***Revive Ministries***

"If you've ever felt that God could love other people but not you, if you've ever felt that God is too distant or too dangerous, you have come to the right place. Lawrence is a very precious brother in Christ. He has a tender heart for people and a passionate heart for Jesus; both born out of his experience with God's tender mercies toward him, as well as his experience in seeing others encounter the same healing that has so renovated his own life. This book is not only a wonderful story, it's a pathway forward. The insights and encounters Lawrence shares will prepare you for your own encounter as you follow the Heart Work invitations that accompany each chapter. It is my prayer that as you read and reflect, you will discover the same tender mercies that have blessed Lawrence's life, and find yourself being equipped to minister your personal healing experience into the life of others."

Dr Allan Meyer - *Founder **Careforce Lifekeys***

"This book takes the reader on a profound and sometimes turbulent road to live in freedom! While sharing his own compelling life story, Lawrence explores its essential elements honestly, clearly, and poetically. He writes reflectively, offering a wealth of practical processes and resources for reflection, based sensitively in lived life experiences and ministry examples. But this is not Lawrence's story alone. He challenges the reader throughout, in their own personal processes, in opening out theological perspectives as well as professional and ministry arenas. While his naming of the persons of the Trinity is strongly gendered, this is deeply consistent with Lawrence's particular journey. He also raises significant contextual issues for ministry formation and critical reflection on practice. Throughout this story there is a prophetic voice that cannot be ignored, and which is steeped in love."

The Rev'd Dr Cecilia Francis -
Professional Supervisor & Spiritual Director

"What is captivating about this book is not merely its title, but also its presentation and the personal stories shared with rawness and honesty. The book is highly accessible to all readers, as they can easily connect with the author's experiences, which are presented in an engaging and spacious style underpinned by solid, easy-to-understand theology and spirituality. The book is filled with various emotions, life-giving energy, and a healing touch demonstrated through Lawrence's challenging and intimate life experiences. It touches on the important issue of the father-son relationship, a deeply impactful aspect of men's lives. This is not a book to read for academic purposes or for leisure like a novel; rather, it is a book of reflection, inviting the reader to pause and reflect on their own life experiences and their relationships with themselves, God, and others."

Khoi Nguyen - *Catholic Priest MSC –*
Missionaries of the Sacred Heart*, Lecturer and supervisor at*
Heart of Life Spirituality Centre *Melbourne, Australia*

"The book has been a source of inspiration for me. Over the last 37 years I have been shaped by the works of Richard Rohr, Thomas Merton, Thomas Moore, Joan Chittister, Rowan Williams, and so many of the ancient Mystics — Hildegard of Bingen, Julian of Norwich, Meister Eckhart, Ignatius of Loyola, and Teresa of Avila. The mystical experience of becoming aware of and attending to the inner life, and discovering the Presence of Divine Compassion, has been part of my journey since childhood. What Lawrence presents here is deeply in line with that exploration. My underlying Scripture is Genesis 1, where Essential Goodness is revealed as the gracious gift of the Divine to the whole cosmos, and we as humans are a core part of that Essential Goodness. This book encapsulates one person's human journey that honours not only the discovery of the Divine in the midst of that journey, but the realisation that the Divine Love and Compassion was always there — even when not recognised. I especially commend this book to people in ministry who are struggling with burnout, those exploring the human/divine journey, and those who believe that sin excludes them from Divine Compassion, most definitely those who are caring for the carer."

John Stuart - *Spiritual Director*
& former Catholic priest

"The title of this fabulous book, Outrageous Love – He Never Turned Away, captures not only the story of God's fathering of Lawrence, but Lawrence himself — a man who loves boldly and without reserve! To spend time with him is to glimpse something of God's heart for others, and that same spirit is woven throughout these pages. This book brings together a vulnerable, honest memoir with thoughtful teaching, gently daring the reader to go deeper with God. The story is raw, courageous, and deeply human, tracing a quest for belonging alongside the transforming power of receiving God's scandalous, unconditional acceptance. It reveals a lived theology shaped by love, faith, and healing, and — against all odds — a healed life poured out generously for others. Outrageous."

Annie Layton - *Pastor, Coach, Mentor & Professional Supervisor*

"This book is a timely reminder that a wounded life lived on empty promises of 'sex, drugs and rock'n'roll' is not beyond healing and grounding in relationships with God and others; however impossible that may feel at times. Lawrence's courageous story reflects a common theme of the search for healing, meaning, and purpose in life which can only emerge in the context of becoming self-aware and reflective. From a life of addiction to one of freedom that he never thought possible, Lawrence's book invites us all into the journey of spiritual growth and is a reminder that no life is beyond God's reach."

Damien Peile - Supervisor *& Mentor,* ***The Carmelite Centre Melbourne***

"*Outrageous Love: He Never Turned Away* is a powerful and moving story, grippingly told, of Lawrence's journey towards the discovery of his true identity as a beloved child of God. Wonderfully honest, readable and engaging, it will be a great healing resource for many. I also love the structure and format of each chapter, the breath prayers and soaking exercises, and also the idea of 'prophetic leaking'. The soaking exercises reminded me of St John Vianney, who said that when we pray we plunge into a bath of love, and also

St Teresa of Avila, who described the highest stage of prayer as God pouring his soaking rain (grace) on us without any effort on our part.I warmly commend *Outrageous Love* as an authentic and inspiring faith journey and witness to the power of God's infinite and unconditional love."

Roland Ashby - *Author, Spiritual Director, Meditation Teacher, Retreat Leader and Contributing Editor of "Living Water"*

"To believe in an ever-present and loving God in our era — where people struggle to believe that truth can be found at all, let alone experienced — seems fraught with disappointment at best and despair at worst. In laying bare the vicissitudes of his own extraordinary pathway to God, Lawrence Prasad encourages and challenges the reader to hold fast to this belief in a God who, against all odds, loves us unconditionally. Prasad's profoundly personal story and the journey he takes us on within that story — through Heart Work reflection, focused meditation, journalling, prayer, and praise — unlocks a door for the possibility of profound encounter with God who is and always has been with us; a door that leads to the acceptance of the true self; and a door that opens out with Good News so urgently needed in our broken world. This work is a culmination of a Spiritual Director's own experience of struggle and spiritual practice."

Dr Carmel Posa - *SGS - Good Samaritan Sister; BSc, GradDipND, GradDipEd(Sec), BTh, MA (Monastic Studies), PhD*

FOREWORD

I have known Lawrence for many years — long enough to have seen not just the public version of his story, but the private wrestlings, the questions asked in quiet moments, and the perseverance required to keep moving forward when turning back would have been easier. Our connection was forged not through theory or shared ideas alone, but through life — through conversations, shared spaces, and moments where the realities of pain, hope, and faith were unmistakably present. I wasn't merely an observer of this journey; often, I was in the room.

What has always stood out to me about Lawrence is not simply what he has survived, but how he has survived it. In him, I see something rare and deeply compelling: the heart of the Father expressed through integrity, love, patience, and understanding. I see a man who refuses to give up — no matter the size, strength, or persistence of the obstacles and opposition before him. His life reflects a powerful, steady attitude of perseverance, rooted not in denial of pain, but in honest engagement with it.

This book tells the story of a little boy with a vision — a vision that life would hold meaning, safety, and love. It is also the story of that same boy becoming even smaller under the weight of abandonment and abuse. It follows a teenager searching desperately for purpose and belonging, asking the questions many ask but few are brave enough to voice. And it traces the long, often difficult journey toward answers — answers that did not come easily or quickly, but were found through courage, faith, and an unwillingness to quit.

This story matters because it is real. It is not polished or packaged for comfort. It is a lived experience, told with honesty, candour, and at times, raw reality. Lawrence does not write from a distance; he writes from within the story. That is precisely why this book will resonate so deeply with those who find themselves living in similar circumstances — those searching for answers, meaning, and a way forward when the path ahead feels unclear or impossible.

By choosing to share his life in this way, Lawrence has taken a significant risk. He has risked misunderstanding, judgment, and vulnerability for the sake of truth. Yet he does so with a clear purpose: to show his readers that no matter where they have come from, they too can find a way forward. His story stands as living testimony that healing is possible, purpose can be rediscovered, and love — outrageous, persistent love — never turns away.

I encourage you to read this book slowly and carefully. Sit with it. Reflect on it. Engage fully with the exercises woven throughout its pages. They are not add-ons or afterthoughts; they are invitations — opportunities to pause, to listen, and to begin discovering your own path toward healing and restoration. If you allow it, this book can become more than something you read; it can become something you experience.

Lawrence's journey is unique, but its implications are for all. His life reminds us that even in the presence of deep wounds and unanswered questions, hope remains. Love remains. And there is always a way forward.

Pastor John Arnott -
*Co-Director of Restore – A **Catch The Fire** Ministry*
(Fondly known as Aussie John in the
***Catch The Fire** Movement)*

INTRODUCTION

An invitation to read this as a story
and a journey

This book is a memoir. It's also a map.

It's a memoir because it tells the truth about my story — the long ache of father wounds, the places of shame and searching, and the slow, surprising way the Father met me with love I couldn't earn and couldn't outrun.

But it's also a map because, along the way, Jesus didn't just rescue me — He re-formed me. He gave me language for what was happening in my heart. He showed me how lies get planted, how shame hides, how the orphan mindset strives, and how beloved identity learns to receive. And later, He taught me how to walk with others in the same gentle, Spirit-led way.

So if, at times, you feel the book 'changes lanes' — from story into teaching, from memoir into ministry — please know it's intentional. I'm not stepping away from the story. I'm showing you what was happening underneath it, and what the Father was building in me as

He healed me.

You can read this book in two ways.

You can read it simply as a story — follow the narrative, let it carry you, and notice what stirs in you along the way.

Or you can read it as a journey — slow down, pause often, and engage with the Heart Work invitations at the end of each chapter.

There's no 'right' way to read it. There's only the way that is kind to your nervous system, honest to your pace, and faithful to what the Holy Spirit is doing in you.

If you're carrying trauma, shame, or father wounds, I want to say this clearly: you are not behind. Healing is not a race. And God is not in a hurry.

A Note About Heart Work Invitations

At the end of each chapter, you'll find a **Heart Work** section — a space for reflection, prayer, and encounter. These aren't just questions to answer; they're invitations to engage with the Father, to let Jesus into your story, and to experience the Holy Spirit's comfort and guidance.

Each Heart Work section includes:

- Scripture to ground you in God's Word
- Reflection Questions to help you process the chapter
- A Journal Prompt with space to write
- One Thing to Try This Week — a simple, practical step
- A Breath Prayer — a short phrase to carry with you
- A Soaking Exercise — an invitation to encounter Jesus in your story
- A Closing Prayer — to gather it all and offer it back to God

Take your time. Go at your own pace. Let this be a safe space for your heart to heal.

You don't have to do every exercise in every chapter. Follow the Holy Spirit's leading. Some sections will resonate deeply; others you may return to later. This is your journey, and the Father is patient.

A Gentle Word About Safety

This book includes themes of trauma, abuse, sexuality, addiction, and shame. Please go gently. If you feel overwhelmed, it's okay to pause, skip ahead, or reach out for support from a trusted friend, pastor, counsellor, or spiritual director. Needing support is not failure — it's wisdom. My prayer is simple: that as you read, you would discover what I discovered — He never turned away.

OPENING QUOTE

"God is good and only good. He has always and only ever been good, and always, only ever been good in EXACTLY the way Jesus revealed."

— **Dubb Alexander**

PART I

HUNGER, WOUNDING AND THE LONG WAY AROUND

PREFACE

Before you begin, a gentle note: some chapters include references to trauma, abuse, addiction, and shame. I've written with care and I won't be graphic, but your body may still remember what your mind has tried to file away. If you feel activated as you read, please pause. Take a breath. Put the book down for a moment. Reach out to someone safe. And if you need more support, it can be wise to speak with a doctor, counsellor, psychologist, or a trauma-informed therapist. You don't have to do this alone.

I want to say this gently: this book contains real stories from my life, including experiences of trauma, shame, addiction, and sexual abuse. I've written with restraint, but some moments may still feel confronting. Please go at your own pace. You're free to pause, skip ahead, or put the book down and come back later. There is no "right" way to read a story like this.

Part I is the beginning of my journey, the early shaping, the hunger underneath the hunger, and the places where wounding took root. It's not a neat origin story, and it's not written to blame or to sensationalise. It's written because what we don't name often continues to name us.

In these chapters you'll see a boy trying to make sense of the world, searching for safety, belonging, and love. You'll also see the long way round: the coping strategies, the false refuges, the inner vows, the ways we learn to survive when we don't yet know how to be held.

If you've ever carried father wounds, felt unseen, or tried to find comfort in places that couldn't truly give it, you may recognise yourself here. My hope is not that you'll simply relate to my pain, but that you'll feel less alone in your own.

And I want you to know this from the start: Part I is not the whole story. It is the honest beginning, but it is not the final word.

As you read, I invite you to listen for the deeper thread beneath the events: the quiet longing for home. The hunger for a love that doesn't turn away.

THE LITTLE POPE

I was the kid who wanted to be the Pope.

Not a priest. Not a bishop. Not the Archbishop or a Cardinal.

The Pope.

If I was going to serve God, I was going all in.

Growing Up in a Charismatic Catholic Home

I was born in Australia into a Catholic family shaped by the Catholic Charismatic Renewal. My mum, Pearl, and my Aunty Wendy were both Spirit-filled, praying women. They took me most Friday evenings to the Sacre Coeur Prayer Community in Melbourne. They didn't just talk about God; they talked to Him. They prayed in tongues while cooking dinner. They worshipped in the lounge room. They laid hands on us when we were sick.

They were my earliest intercessors, my first teachers of prayer, and living examples of what it looked like to love Jesus with everything.

Names like John and Paula Sandford from Elijah House Ministries floated around our house. Inner healing, forgiveness, and the work of the Holy Spirit weren't strange concepts; they were part of the air we breathed. There was an expectation that God was real, that the Holy Spirit was active, and that prayer could actually change things.

And I believed it.

The Little Pope

As a child, I had an intense hunger for God.

While other kids were playing with their GI-Joe superheroes, I was playing Mass.

I'd line up my little Jesus figurines, Jesus the little infant, Jesus the Redeemer and my favourite the Sacred Heart of Jesus and some saints as well, setting up elaborate scenes of worship and devotion on the card table. I'd drape towels or tea towels over my shoulders like vestments, fashioning a chasuble my great grandma Eva had made for me in this glorious gold fabric, and process around the house with all the seriousness of a Vatican procession.

I even created a home confessional in the back shed.

I'd drag a chair into the corner, sit behind it, and insist that family members come and 'confess' their sins to me. My mum and Aunty Wendy would humour me, whispering made-up confessions while I solemnly offered absolution and made the sign of the cross.

It was funny, yes, but it was also sincere.

I wasn't playing at being powerful. This all came from a simple thought: who is the closest person to God? The Pope.

I wanted to be holy.
I wanted to be set apart.
I wanted to be His.

I wanted to be close to God.

Looking back now, I can see that hunger was planted by the Father Himself. It was His fingerprint on my life, even before I understood what it meant.

Early Whispers of the Father

There were moments, even as a little boy, when I sensed something more than religion.

I remember lying in bed at night, staring at the ceiling, talking to God in the dark. Not formal prayers, just childlike conversations:

> "God, are You there?"
> "Do You see me?"
> "Do You like me?"

Sometimes, in those quiet moments, I felt a warmth in my chest, a sense of being watched over. I didn't have language yet for 'the Father's love,' but I knew I wasn't alone.

In church, I'd feel waves of emotion during worship or when the priest lifted the host. I didn't understand doctrine; I just knew something holy was happening and I wanted to be as close to it as possible.

The seeds were there:

- A longing to belong to God.
- A sensitivity to His presence.
- A desire to serve and be set apart.

The Father was already at work, drawing my heart.

As a four-year-old walking to kindergarten the only way my mum Pearl could teach me to count was including God into a rhyme. She would sing with her most tender and well-spoken voice:

One, Two, Three, Four, Five, thank God I'm alive,

Six, Seven, Eight, Nine, Ten, I'm thanking Him again,

Eleven, Twelve, Thirteen, Fourteen, Fifteen, thank God my Spirit's lifting,

Sixteen, Seventeen, Eighteen, Nineteen, Twenty, thank God I've got plenty.

When Hunger Meets Pain

But hunger doesn't exempt you from pain.

Very early on, cracks began to form in the world I knew, family fractures, confusion, and wounds that I'll unpack more in later chapters. The simple, bright world of the 'little Pope' started to get complicated.

The same sensitivity that made me aware of God also made me deeply aware of rejection, shame, and the feeling of not being wanted. The world stopped feeling safe. My own heart stopped feeling safe.

Slowly, the hunger for God that had once been so pure and simple began to get buried under layers of:

- pain I didn't know how to process;
- questions I didn't know how to ask; and
- coping mechanisms that promised comfort but delivered more emptiness.

For many years, I forgot that little boy in the makeshift vestments.

I forgot the joy of lining up figurines and pretending to bless them.
I forgot the nights of whispering to God in the dark.
I forgot the innocence of wanting nothing more than to be close to Him.

But the Father never forgot.

The Hunger Never Really Left

Even in the darkest seasons of my life, and there were many, that hunger never fully left.

It was buried.
It was distorted.
It was redirected toward things that could never satisfy.

But it was still there, like an ember under ash.

When I chased spirituality in other religions, it was that hunger. When I threw myself into the club and drag scene, it was that hunger. When I numbed myself with substances and performance, it was that hunger trying to find a home.

I thought I was searching for identity, belonging, and affirmation.

Underneath it all, I was searching for the Father.

The Father's Story

This book is, on one level, my story — of trauma, searching, encounter, and healing.

But more than that, it's the Father's story.

The story of a Father who never stopped pursuing the little boy who wanted to be the Pope, even when that boy grew into a man who ran in the opposite direction.

The story of a Father who loved me:

- in the confusion of childhood;
- in the hidden pain of abuse and abandonment;
- in the temples of other gods; and
- in the clubs, the drag persona, the addiction, the shame.

The story of a Father who waited patiently, not with crossed arms and a tapping foot, but with open arms and aching heart, for the day I would finally be ready to receive what He'd been offering all along:

His outrageous love.

The hunger that burned in the 'little Pope' was never ultimately about religion, ritual, or even ministry.

It was for Him.

For the Father's embrace.
For the Father's voice.
For the Father's outrageous, scandalous, unconditional love that never gives up, never runs out, never fails.

That's the journey you're about to read.

And as you walk through my story, my prayer is that you'll begin to recognise your own:

- the places where the Father planted hunger;
- the places where pain buried it; and
- the ways He's been quietly, faithfully, outrageously loving you all along.

HEART WORK

Reflection, Prayer, and Encounter

Scripture

"I knew you before I formed you in your mother's womb. Before you were born I set you apart and appointed you."

— Jeremiah 1:5 (TPT)

Reflection Questions

Choose 1-3 questions that stand out to you today. You don't need to answer them all.

If you're reading in a group, you may choose one question to share and keep the rest private.

- What was your first encounter with God's presence? How did it shape your understanding of who He is?
- Where do you see God's fingerprints in your childhood, even in moments you didn't recognise Him at the time?
- What does "childlike faith" look like for you today? Where have you lost that simplicity?
- What hunger has God planted in your heart? Is it still alive, or has it been buried?
- Can you identify a time when God was pursuing you, even when you didn't realise it?

Journal Prompt

"Father, the hunger You planted in my heart as a child was..."

Take 5–10 minutes to write freely. Don't edit or overthink, just let your heart speak.

Your Reflections:

____

____

____

____

____

____

____

One Thing to Try This Week

Sit quietly for 5 minutes and ask, "Father, where were You in my childhood?" Write down whatever comes to mind, an image, a feeling, a memory, or simply silence. Don't force it; just notice.

Breath Prayer for This Week

Inhale: "You knew me"
Exhale: "before I was born"

Repeat this throughout your day, in the car, before bed, during a walk. Let it settle into your heart.

Soaking Exercise

Encountering Jesus in Your Childhood

1. Find a quiet space. Put on instrumental worship music or sit in silence.

2. Close your eyes and take a few deep breaths. Invite the Holy Spirit to lead you.

3. Picture yourself as a child, whatever age comes to mind. Notice where you are, what you're wearing, how you feel.

4. Ask Jesus, "Where were You in this moment?"

5. Wait quietly. Don't rush or force an answer. Notice any images, feelings, words, or sensations that surface.

6. If nothing comes, that's okay. Simply rest in His presence. He is with you now.

7. When you're ready, thank Him for being present, then and now.

What did you notice?

Prayer

Father,
Thank You that You knew me before I was born.
You saw me in my childhood,
in the moments of wonder and the moments of wounding.

I invite You into my earliest experiences and memories.
Show me where You were present, even when I didn't see You.
Awaken the hunger You planted in my heart.

Help me to see myself the way You see me,
set apart, known, and loved from the very beginning.

Restore the simplicity and wonder of a child who knows they are
safe with You.

Let it be so,

Amen.

CHAPTER 2

WHEN FATHERS LEAVE

Content warning: This chapter contains descriptions of childhood trauma, sexual abuse, and family dysfunction. Please proceed with care. If you are affected, please seek professional help.

The foundation of my story, the wound that would shape everything, began before I was even born.

We often think our story starts with our first breath.

Mine started in the womb.

Prenatal Wounds

I didn't have language for 'prenatal wounds' until years later, through prayer ministry and honest conversations with my mum. But once I did, so much of my life suddenly made sense.

My mum was forty-two when she became pregnant with me. She already had two daughters and wasn't sure she could handle another child at her age. She was tired. Life was complicated. The idea of starting again with a baby felt overwhelming.

She wasn't cold or unloving, just uncertain, hesitant, and reserved about the pregnancy.

My dad, on the other hand, was excited. He wanted a son.

Two very different emotional realities. And as we now know, a baby in the womb is not a blank slate. We are deeply sensitive to the emotional climate around us, our brains might not be fully formed, but our hearts are little receptors, retaining all that occurs around us.

My mum's uncertainty, her fear, her "I don't know if I can do this" were not just thoughts in her head. They became the emotional atmosphere I swam in before I had words.

And in that atmosphere, a lie was planted in me before I ever saw the light of day:

"I'm not sure if I'm wanted. I don't really belong."

That lie became the lens through which I would see the world for decades. It became the foundation for every later experience of rejection, abandonment, and not being enough.

When Fathers Leave

When I was six years old, my parents divorced.

My dad remarried and started a new life. A new house. A new family. A new chapter.

And I was left behind.

Not with a dramatic speech or a slammed door. Just a slow, painful drift. Phone calls became less frequent and visits less consistent. I had a sense that I was no longer central to his world.

There's one memory that cemented the wound of abandonment in my heart.

My dad promised to pick me up after school.

I remember waiting at my front door after school with my little bag. The light started to fade.

I waited.

And waited.

And waited.

He never came.

I waited into the evening, still believing he would show up. Still believing he wouldn't forget me. Children are slow to give up hope.

But he didn't come.

Eventually, after falling asleep my mum woke me up. And I realised he never came for me.

On the inside, something hardened.

The lie that had been planted in the womb crystallised into a belief:

> "I'm not worth showing up for.
> I'm not worth remembering.
> I'm not worth keeping."

That belief didn't just sit in my mind; it sank into my bones.

Before I take you into the next part of my story, I want to offer a clear warning and a gentle pause. The next pages include references to sexual abuse. I won't describe anything graphically, but I will be honest. If you need to stop here, please do. Take a breath. You're safe. And if this touches your own story, consider reading the next section with support.

The Silence of Abuse

Between the ages of six and twelve, I was sexually molested by five different individuals.

It started with a friend, another boy my age. I didn't recognise this as molestation, but it was. My friend had been abused by a boy just a little older than him. This boy had been abused by his friend the same age who had been abused by a neighbour who was later identified as a paedophile. Abuse moved through that little network of boys like a generational trauma, affecting at least five of us that I know of.

At the time, it didn't feel like 'assault' in the way we talk about it now.

It felt like:

- Attention.
- Connection.
- Being chosen.

When you already believe you're not wanted, any form of being noticed can feel like love.

But underneath, more lies were being planted:

> "This is what love looks like.
> This is what connection feels like.
> This is my fault.
> I'm dirty.
> I'm broken.
> I'm fundamentally flawed."

One of my later abusers was an adult male. During a stay with my father's new wife's family, he molested me. That experience added a new layer of confusion, shame, and fear. If adults, those who are supposed to protect you, cross those lines, what does that say about your worth?

I never told anyone.

I didn't have the language. I couldn't make sense of what was happening. I couldn't reconcile the strange mixture of feeling wanted and feeling deeply wrong.

So, I did what many abused children do:

I turned the pain inward.

Building a Fortress

When everything else felt out of control, I found one thing I could control: food.

Eating became a comfort.

Food became a friend that didn't leave, didn't abuse, didn't forget.

I began to build a fortress around myself with my own body.

By the age of twelve, I was morbidly obese, around 122 kilos. My size became a shield, a way to disappear and be seen at the same time. If I was big enough, maybe people would stop touching me. If I was big enough, maybe I could hide.

Depression wrapped itself around me like a heavy blanket. I refused to go to school. Child Protective Services became involved. My beautiful mum tried everything — doctors, psychologists, counsellors. She did everything a loving mother could do.

But nothing could touch the internal devastation.

What I needed wasn't just another professional.

I needed a father's love.

My Dad, Hari

My relationship with my father, Hari, was complicated.

There were good memories — watching wrestling together, Saturday market trips, and eating curry and doughnuts. These were moments of connection I clung to like precious stones.

After the divorce, after his remarriage, after the new life, those moments became fewer and further between. The gap between us widened. The wounds deepened.

For years, I carried anger towards my dad. Resentment. Bitterness. A sense of, "You left me. You chose them over me. You didn't fight for me."

Later, as my healing journey began, I started to learn his story.

Hari was a third-generation descendant of indentured labourers from Basti District, Uttar Pradesh, India, taken to Fiji. His childhood was marked by poverty, instability, and abandonment. At eight years old, he was placed in a boys' home.

He was never fathered.

He carried his own father wound — raw, unhealed, unspoken. He struggled with alcoholism. He did the best he knew how, with the tools he had. But here's the painful truth:

You can't give away what you've never received.

He hadn't received fathering.

So, he couldn't father me.

That doesn't excuse the pain. But it helps explain it.

Breaking the Generational Cycle

Understanding my dad's story didn't erase what happened to me. It didn't magically heal the missed pick-ups, the absence, the ache.

But it did something important; it gave me compassion.

I began to see him not as a one-dimensional villain, but as a wounded man — a little boy inside an adult body — doing the best he could with a broken toolkit.

And it gave me a choice.

Would I continue the cycle of fatherlessness, passing the same wounds down to the next generation? Or would I, by the grace of God, break it?

I chose to break it.

Not because I'm strong or particularly noble, but because I encountered the Father's love.

His love gave me the power to:

- forgive;
- release;
- honour my dad for what he did give; and
- grieve what he couldn't give.

Along the way, God brought other fathers into my life.

I honour Peter Sharp, my foster father, who stepped in during critical years with love, boundaries, and stability.

I honour John Arnott (Aussie John) and other spiritual fathers who showed me, in flesh and blood, what a good father looks like — steady, kind, present.

And above all, I honour my heavenly Father, who fathered me when no one else could.

The Cycle Stops Here

The cycle of fatherlessness doesn't get the final word in my family.

Not for me.
Not for my nephew Jordan.
Not for my nieces Grace and Amelia.
Not for the next generation.

They will know what it feels like to be fathered well.
They will know whose they are.
They will know they are loved, wanted, valued, and cherished.
That's the fruit of healing.

Not pretending the past didn't happen.
Not minimising the pain.

But allowing the Father's love to come into the deepest wounds —
prenatal, childhood, generational — and write a different story.

HEART WORK

Reflection, Prayer, and Encounter

Scripture

"Even if my father and mother abandon me, the Lord will hold me close."

— Psalm 27:10 (NLT)

"Even if my father and mother would forsake me, Yahweh will gather me up and adopt me as his very own child."

— Psalm 27:10 (Mirror Bible)

Reflection Questions

Choose 1-3 questions that stand out to you today. You don't need to answer them all.

If you're reading in a group, you may choose one question to share and keep the rest private.

- How has your relationship with your earthly father (or lack thereof) shaped your view of God the Father?
- What lies have you believed about God because of wounds from your past?
- Do you sense you might be carrying a prenatal or early-life wound? What lie might have been planted there?
- Have you experienced sexual abuse or molestation? Have you ever spoken about it in a safe space?

- What lies have you believed about yourself because of abuse or trauma?
- What generational patterns or cycles of pain can you see in your family story?
- Can you look at your parent(s) with compassion, recognising the wounds they carried?
- What generational cycle is God inviting you to break?

Journal Prompt

"The absence or presence of my father taught me that God is…"

Write honestly. Let yourself name the lies you've believed, and then ask the Father, "What is the truth?"

Your Reflections:

One Thing to Try This Week

Write a letter to your earthly father (you don't have to send it). Tell him what you needed, what you didn't receive, and how it affected you. Then ask Jesus, "Where were You when my father left or failed me?"

Breath Prayer for This Week

Inhale: "You will never leave me"
Exhale: "You hold me close"

Let this truth settle deeper than the wound.

Soaking Exercise

Inviting the Father into the Absence

1. Find a quiet space and invite the Holy Spirit to guide you.
2. Close your eyes and picture a moment when you felt abandoned, rejected, or alone — especially connected to your father or a father figure.
3. Don't rush past the pain. Let yourself feel it.
4. Now ask, "Father, where were You in that moment?"
5. Wait. Notice what comes — an image, a word, a feeling, or simply His presence.
6. If you see or sense Him there, ask, "What do You want me to know?"
7. Rest in whatever He shows you. Thank Him for never leaving, even when others did.

What did you notice?

Prayer

Father,
You know the wounds I carry from my earthly father —
the absence, the words, the silence, the harm.

I bring those wounds to You now.

Show me where You were when I felt most alone.
Speak truth over the lies I believed about myself and about You.

Heal the father wound in my heart.
May I learn to know what it means to be held, seen, and loved by
You —
not because I earned it, but because I am Yours.

Break the generational cycles of pain in my family.
Let healing begin with me.

I choose to forgive my father (or father figure) —
not because it didn't hurt,
but because I don't want to carry this anymore.

Hold me close, Father.
I am Your beloved child.

Let it be so,

Amen.

CHAPTER 3

SEARCHING IN THE DARKNESS

When you don't know who you are, you'll search for identity anywhere.

And I searched everywhere.

The ache that began as a prenatal wound and deepened through abuse and abandonment didn't disappear as I grew older. It just changed shape. The little boy who wanted to be the Pope grew into a teenager who felt lost, angry, and painfully alone.

I was still hungry for God. I just didn't know who He was anymore, or if He wanted me.

Hinduism: Six Years of Searching

Disconnected from the God I'd known as a child and desperate for belonging, during my adolescence I became a prayerful Hindu for six years.

Hinduism drew me in with its sense of openness and inclusivity, the idea that there are many paths to the divine, many names for God, many ways to reach the sacred. Compared to the version of Christianity I'd experienced — exclusive, rule-heavy, and often judgemental — it felt safer.

In Hinduism, I didn't feel like I had to fit into a narrow box. There was room for mystery, for questions, for a sense of the spiritual that wasn't constantly measuring me and finding me lacking.

So, I threw myself in.

I learned prayers and mantras. I participated in rituals. I honoured deities. I lit incense and offered devotion. I wasn't playing games; I was sincere. I wanted to connect with God — whoever He was and however He might reveal Himself.

But underneath the rituals, the same emptiness remained.

I began to realise that what I was searching for wasn't:

- a religion;
- a set of practices; or
- a belief system.

I was searching for a Father.

I didn't have language for that yet, but my heart did.

The Club Scene: A World That Felt Like Home

At seventeen, my best friend came out as gay and invited me to a gay club in Melbourne called Three Faces.

The moment I walked in, something in me relaxed with a sense of familiarity.

The lights were dim, the music was loud, people were dancing, and there was electricity in the air. People were laughing, flirting, dancing, embracing. There was a sense of freedom, of 'come as you are,' that I hadn't felt in church for a long time.

It didn't feel foreign.
It didn't feel threatening.

It felt familiar.

Because of the abuse I'd experienced as a child, the environment, the affection, the attention, the sexualised atmosphere felt like home. Bizarre, yes. But familiar. My nervous system recognised it before my mind did.

I started going regularly. Week after week, the club became my sanctuary. The dance floor became my altar. The people there became my congregation.

Eventually, I was introduced to the drag scene.

MizDomina: The Persona That Became My Identity

I created a drag persona: **MizDomina**.

She was everything I wasn't.

Confident.
Bold.
Untouchable.
Celebrated.
Loved.

As MizDomina, I could walk into a room and own it. I could command attention, make people laugh, shock them, entertain them. I could be larger than life, and for a few hours, the little boy who felt unwanted and broken could disappear.

In the late 90's the drag scene in Melbourne was prestigious — elaborate costumes, choreography, inside jokes, a unique culture all of its own. I was good at it. I worked hard at my craft and was celebrated for it.

And there were genuinely fun moments — creativity, community, laughter, the thrill of performing. I'm grateful for the many friendships and wonderful memories.

But MizDomina was also a mask.

She was a way to escape the pain.
A way to be someone else.
A way to avoid the parts of me that still felt unlovable.

The more I performed, the more disconnected I became from my true self. The applause was loud, but the silence afterwards was louder. When the makeup came off and the lights went down, I was still Lawrence, still carrying the same wounds, the same lies, the same ache.

Drugs and the Underworld

At seventeen, I was introduced to ecstasy at the Monkey rave party at The Palace in St Kilda.

The feelings of love, connection, and euphoria were powerful. For a few hours, the emptiness seemed to disappear. The music pulsed through my body, strangers became friends, and the world felt bright and possible.

But it was counterfeit. MDMA was a counterfeit of feeling loved, so now it makes so much sense why, week after week, drugs were taken as we chased wanting to feel loved.

By nineteen, I wasn't just taking drugs. I was involved in that world, moving in circles across multiple clubs, expanding my reach, becoming a trusted contact.

Looking back now, I can see something I couldn't see then.

This was a **perversion** of the leadership, influence, and stewardship God had placed in me.

The very gifts God would later redeem: organisation, connection, the ability to gather people, were being used to build a system of darkness instead of a kingdom of light.

But even in the darkness, God was there.

Waiting.
Watching.
Loving.

Same Sex Attraction: An Invitational Message to the Church

I want to talk about my experience with same sex attraction with deep humility. This is **my** story, not a template or prescription for anyone else.

I honour my many friends in the LGBTQ+ community, some of whom I consider family. I reject the 'us vs them' mentality that has caused so much harm. I'm not interested in weaponising theology against people made in the image of God.

What I am interested in is love.

For me, same sex attraction was woven together with:

- childhood abuse;
- a desperate need for male affirmation; and
- a longing to be seen, chosen, and held.

That doesn't mean everyone's story is the same. It simply means that in my life, sexuality, trauma, and identity were deeply entangled.

To the Church, I want to say this:

Please don't fixate on debating sin or positions while ignoring people's pain.

Jesus has already dealt with sin at the cross and torn down the wall of separation. The illusion that we are 'in' and others are 'out' must be broken so that love can flow freely.

Repentance — *metanoia* — is not about shame. It's about transformation. It's a kingdom upgrade: a change of mind, heart, spirit, and direction in response to love, not fear.

I often come back to the image of the prodigal father's extravagant love. I want to share a significant moment when I sensed the Trinity speak directly to my heart:

"Lawrence, my son, if you ever draw religious lines or withdraw love to conditions, I will stand with those on the other side of your line and invite you to 'cross over' and to join Me in loving more." As it was all over at the cross.

Jesus never left me or was ashamed of me during my years in the clubs and the drag scene. He walked with me into those spaces, sat with me in my mess, and loved me in the middle of it all.

The central question of my life is not "Did you get everything right?"

The question is:

"Did you learn to love — and how well did you love?"

Did You Learn to Love?

This part of my story is an invitation to the Church to love well.

To:

- honour feelings and emotions as real and important, not enemies to be suppressed;
- let kindness, not condemnation lead people to transformation; and
- break the illusion of separation and recognise that we are all beloved children of the Father, whether we know it yet or not.

I'm not asking you to agree with every detail of my journey.

I'm asking:

- Can we love well?
- Can we refuse to dehumanise people whose stories we don't fully understand?
- Can we let the Father's love flow without barriers, trusting Him to do the deep work in people's hearts?

That's the invitation.

Not to win arguments.
Not to draw lines.
Not to determine who's in and who's out.

But to love.

Because love is a Person.
Love is an embrace.
Love is who we are.
Love is how we were formed.
Love is how we were created.
Love is where we belong.

We are loved, and we are made from Love, for Love.

The False Self

MizDomina became the beautiful mask that allowed me to escape my pain.

Yes, there were real moments of joy, creativity, and connection. I'm genuinely thankful for some of those experiences and friendships discovered with my alter-ego.

But when I started to get honest with myself, I had to admit:

Towards the end, the more I performed, the more disconnected I became from my true self.

The applause and affirmation, as amazing as they were, could not fill the deep void left by my father's absence and the wounds of abuse. They were like sugar — sweet in the moment, but leaving me emptier afterwards.

I was searching for identity in all the wrong places.

But the Father had another plan.

He had always had another plan.

The same God who watched over the 'little Pope', who wept with the abused child, who walked beside the Hindu devotee, and who stood with me on the dance floor was quietly, patiently, leading me toward a different kind of life.

A life where I wouldn't have to perform to be loved.
A life where I wouldn't have to hide behind personas.
A life where my deepest hunger for identity, belonging, and love would finally be met in the Father's embrace.

HEART WORK

Reflection, Prayer, and Encounter

Scripture

"Where could I go from your Spirit? Where could I run and hide from your face? If I go up to heaven, you're there! If I go down to the realm of the dead, you're there too! ... Even in darkness I cannot hide from you."

— Psalm 139:7–8, 12b (TPT)

Reflection Questions

Choose 1-3 questions that stand out to you today. You don't need to answer them all.

If you're reading in a group, you may choose one question to share and keep the rest private.

- Where have you searched for identity, love, and belonging outside of God?
- What 'false selves' or personas have you created to feel accepted?
- Have you ever felt like you had to perform to be loved? Where did that belief come from?
- What does it mean to you that Jesus was present in your darkest moments, not condemning but loving?
- How do you respond to the idea that feelings and emotions matter in the context of sexuality and identity?

- Have you drawn lines that Jesus is inviting you to cross — people you've excluded or judged?

- How well have you loved? Not, How right have you been? But, How well have you loved?

Journal Prompt

"The darkest place I've searched for love was…and what I was really looking for was…"

Be honest. Name the clubs, the substances, the relationships, the personas. Then ask Jesus, "Where were You there?"

Your Reflections:

One Thing to Try This Week

Think of one 'false self' or mask you've worn (the performer, the rebel, the perfect one, the invisible one). Ask Jesus, "What were You trying to protect by wearing this mask?" and "Who am I underneath it?"

Breath Prayer for This Week

Inhale: "Even in darkness"
Exhale: "You are with me"

Let this truth reach the places you thought He could never go.

Soaking Exercise
Jesus in Your Darkest Place

1. Find a quiet, safe space. Invite the Holy Spirit to lead you gently.

2. Close your eyes and picture one of the darkest seasons or places in your story — a club, a relationship, an addiction, a secret.

3. Don't judge yourself. Just notice: What were you searching for? What did you need?

4. Now ask Jesus, "Were You there? Where were You?"

5. Wait. Let Him show you. He may be sitting beside you, weeping with you, or holding you.

6. Ask Him, "What do You want me to know about that time?"

7. Receive whatever He offers — comfort, truth, or simply His presence.

What did you notice?

Prayer

Jesus,
You know the places I've searched for love in all the wrong ways.
You know the masks I've worn, the personas I've created,
the darkness I've hidden in.

Thank You that You were there,
not condemning, not distant, but present and loving.

I invite You into those places now.
Show me what I was really searching for.
Show me the unmet needs beneath the behaviour.

Heal the shame that says I went too far,
that I'm too broken, too dirty, too much.

May I learn there is no place so dark
that Your love cannot reach me there.

Help me to see myself and others,
not by how 'right' we've been,
but by how well we've loved.

I am Yours, even in the darkness.

Let it be so.

Amen.

THE TWELVE-YEAR JOURNEY

Transformation doesn't happen overnight.

At least, it didn't for me.

For a long time, I thought real Christians had dramatic 'before and after' stories: one encounter, one altar call, one moment where everything changed and they never struggled again.

My story didn't look like that.

Mine was a twelve-year journey of Jesus walking with me in the clubs, in the drag scene, in the drug world, and mess. Patiently, kindly and relentlessly until His love finally broke through every wall I'd built.

Travis and the Little Piece of Paper

I was seventeen when I first noticed him.

I was sneaking into nightclubs back then, living for the lights and the noise. One night I was at The Peel Dance Bar in Collingwood, hanging out with friends, when I saw a guy walk through the club who just felt… different.

Same room, same music, same crowd, but his energy was different.

Later I found out his name was Travis and that he was the lighting technician at the venue. We had little conversations here and there, nothing deep, but there was always something about him I couldn't quite name. In the middle of the gay nightclub world, he carried a peace and a presence that didn't match the atmosphere.

About a year later, I was at my other favourite club: the famous Dome Nightclub on Commercial Road in Melbourne, where the infamous Miss Jane hosted her celebrity bar and people came from everywhere, queuing for hours just to try and get in — most being refused.

This was my Saturday-night home every week for years.

One night I looked up… and there was Travis.

He'd gotten a job at the Dome. Week after week we'd see each other, talk between sets, and laugh about the craziness of the night. Again, his energy was different from everyone else in the space. He was fully present in the club world, but he wasn't swallowed by it.

After one particularly long night working in the clubs, I ended up back at his house. It was early morning, that strange in-between time when the city is quiet and the adrenaline is wearing off. We sat in his room, talking deeply about life, family, faith, and the mess I was in.

At one point he said, "Lawrence, I need to tell you something."

I braced myself. "Okay… what?"

"I'm a Christian," he said.

I laughed. "Yeah, I love Jesus too. Jesus is amazing."

He smiled. "You do love Jesus. But your version of Jesus is a little bit different to mine — different to what I experience."

Then he reached into his wallet and pulled out a tiny, folded piece of paper.

It was the classic salvation prayer.

He handed it to me and said, "Just read this. Don't overthink it. No pressure."

Then he left the room.

I was sitting at his desk, alone, holding this little piece of paper. I unfolded it and looked at the words — and in that moment, the atmosphere in the room shifted.

A heaviness filled the space. It was like the air got thick and dark. I was suddenly consumed with dread.

Thoughts rushed through my mind:

"Lawrence, don't do it. What sort of life is that? You don't want that. You don't want to go back to a one-way faith-based life. Look how much you enjoy your life now. You love the people you're with. You love the party life. You love all the things that make your life feel better. Why would you give that up?"

I felt tormented.

I was only nineteen. Everything in my life was governed by feeling and emotion. If I felt it, I did it. If I desired it, I chased it. There was no wisdom or discernment — just impulse.

Sitting there in that room, I thought, I don't know if I can do this. I don't know if I can abstain from everything I'm enjoying. I don't know if I want to give it up.

What felt like an eternity later, Travis walked back in. He took one look at my face and saw the torment.

"Lawrence," he said gently, "just read the prayer. You've got nothing to lose. Just read it.

"You don't have to stop your life. You don't have to stop doing anything. I'm not telling you to stop the drugs, the partying — anything. Jesus just wants to be part of it. Invite Him into your life as it is. Into the mess. Jesus isn't afraid of the mess. Just invite Him in."

That answer undid me.

All my life I'd believed there was this invisible line between God and me, and I had to drag myself across it by being good enough. In that moment, Travis was saying the opposite.

The line was an illusion.

The veil had already been torn.

Jesus was already near. I just wasn't aware of Him.

"This prayer," he said, "isn't about dragging Jesus into your world. It's about becoming aware that He's already with you."

Then he left the room again.

I was alone with the paper.

I read the prayer once… and nothing happened. No fireworks. No feelings. Just more dread.

The thoughts came rushing back, louder this time:

"See? I told you. No one cares about you. He doesn't love you. He's just like your dad. You're alone. You have to look after yourself. You've done a good job so far — keep doing it. Make it all about you. You don't need anyone."

In the middle of that swirl, I felt the faintest whisper inside:

Put your hand on your heart, Lawrence. Read it one more time.

So I did.

I put my hand on my chest and, slowly, from somewhere deeper within, I prayed:

"Dear Jesus… forgive me. I invite You in."

I was looking down at my jeans as I read, and suddenly I noticed they were wet.

What the heck? I thought. Is there a leak from the ceiling?

I looked up — no water, no rain. Then I touched my face and realised:

I was crying.

I hadn't cried in over eight years. I'd built a dam around my heart and held it shut for dear life. And now, with my hand on my heart and a simple whispered prayer, the dam broke.

Tears poured down my face.

As the tears flowed, it felt like tangible scales fell off my eyes. I blinked and suddenly the room looked different. Light streamed through the window in a way I'd never noticed before. The sky outside looked bluer. The trees looked greener. I could see the individual detail in the leaves — it was creation crying out to me.

It was like I'd been living in a world with the brightness turned down, and someone had just turned it up.

A breeze moved through the room, and the heavy darkness that had pressed in on me vanished.

In that moment, I knew that I had just encountered the person of Love.

Travis walked back in, took one look at my face, and grinned.

"Oh," he said, "you read the prayer."

My countenance had changed. Something in me had shifted. I didn't have language for it yet, but I could see love for what it was.

That moment — in a simple bedroom, with a tiny piece of paper and a hesitant yes — marked the beginning of a twelve-year journey with Jesus. One where He would patiently walk with me through the clubs, through my habits, through my shame, until the orphan tendencies in me finally began to believe:

He never turned away.

Your Little Piece of Paper

You might not be sitting in a friend's bedroom with a folded prayer in your hand, but I wonder if you've ever had a 'little piece of paper' moment.

A moment where you sensed an invitation from God, quiet
but persistent.
A moment where part of you wanted to say yes, and another part
of you was terrified of what it might cost.
A moment where all your fears and lies shouted louder than the
whisper of love.

Maybe you've believed, like I did, that saying yes to Jesus means losing yourself, losing joy, losing colour. Maybe you've thought you had to clean yourself up first, or give up everything you enjoy, before He would come near.

What if the truth is closer to what Travis said to me that day:

Jesus isn't afraid of your mess.
He's not waiting for you on the 'clean' side of the line.
He's already with you, right where you are, waiting for your yes.

You can pray something as simple as:

"Jesus, if You're real… if You actually want me… if You really want to be in my life as it is, then I invite You in.
I don't know how to fix myself. I don't know how to change.
But I put my hand on my heart, and I say:
'Dear Jesus, I invite You into my mess and my life,
Let me see what I've never seen before.
Let me feel what I've been too afraid to feel.
Show me that You've never turned away.'"

The power isn't in perfect words.

It's in the honest yes of your heart.

Twelve Years in the Clubs — with Jesus

Here's what most people don't understand:

After that day at Travis's house, I did not immediately leave the clubs.

For the next twelve years, I continued working in nightclubs. I continued performing in drag. I continued in the drug world. I still lived in the same world, with the same people, doing many of the same things.

But I didn't feel alone anymore.

Jesus was with me in the clubs.

He was with me backstage while I put on makeup and costumes.
He was with me on the dance floor, in the DJ booth, in the quiet moments after everyone went home.
He was with me when I was high, when I was crashing, when I was performing, when I was pretending.

He didn't stand outside the club with a clipboard, waiting to see if I'd behave well enough to earn His presence.

He came inside.

He didn't condemn. He didn't shame. He didn't demand that I clean up before He would love me.

He just loved me.

Patiently. Kindly. Gently.

There were moments, even in that season, where I'd sense His presence so strongly it almost took my breath away. In the middle of a dance set, I'd feel this quiet whisper: "I'm here." Walking home at dawn, mascara smudged, heart aching, I'd feel Him beside me. Not accusing. Not disgusted.

Present.

Sometimes that made me angry. Part of me wanted Him to storm in, flip the tables of my life, and force me to change. Another part of me was terrified He might actually do that. So, I kept running, and He kept walking with me.

Looking back, I can see what He was doing.

He was winning my heart, not just my behaviour.

He was slowly untangling lies:

- that I was too dirty to be loved;
- that my worth depended on my performance; and
- that if God ever came close, it would only be to punish or reject me.

He didn't transform me through condemnation.
He didn't transform me through fear.
He didn't transform me through shame.

He transformed me through love.

Over those twelve years, there were countless small moments, conversations, encounters, and whispers in the night where He gently invited me deeper. He never forced. He never manipulated. He never used fear as a motivator.

He just kept loving me.

And slowly, the things that once felt like life started to lose their grip. The clubs that had once felt like home began to feel hollow. The persona that had once felt powerful began to feel like a costume I couldn't wait to take off.

It didn't happen in a weekend. It didn't happen in a three-step program.

It happened over twelve long, patient, grace-saturated years.

The Difference Between Shame and Conviction

During those twelve years in the clubs, I began to learn something I'd never been taught in church:

The difference between **shame** and **conviction**.

Shame had been my constant companion for as long as I could remember. It sounded like this:

"You're bad. You're disgusting. You're broken. You're a disappointment. Get away from Me."

Shame doesn't just say, "You did something wrong."

Shame says, "You **are** something wrong."

It doesn't offer a way out. It just pushes you further into hiding.

Conviction, on the other hand, has a completely different tone. When the Holy Spirit convicts, it sounds more like:

"You're Mine. You're loved. This behaviour is hurting you and others. Come closer to Me and let Me heal you."

Shame pushes you away from God.
Conviction draws you toward Him.

Shame leaves you stuck in the dark.
Conviction turns on the light and holds out a hand.

Jesus never shamed me.

Not once.

Even in the middle of the clubs, even when I was high, even when I was performing as MizDomina or with drugs, I never heard Him say, "You disgust Me. I'm done with you."

What I did hear, over and over, in a hundred different ways, was:

"Lawrence, this isn't who you really are. You're My son. I have more for you than this. Come closer."

Sometimes that conviction came as a quiet ache after a night out. Sometimes it came as a sudden awareness that what I was doing was costing me more than it was giving me. Sometimes it came through the words of people who loved me.

But it was always wrapped in love.

That's how I learned:

- Shame says, "Change, or you can't come near."
- Conviction says, "Come near, and I'll help you change."

The process was slow, but it was real.

The process was the point.

God wasn't just trying to modify my behaviour. He was after my heart. And hearts don't heal overnight.

His transformation in me was slow, deep, and lasting.

A Prophetic Mother Steps In

One of the turning points in that twelve-year journey came when God sent a prophetic mother into my life. I didn't know it then, but her words would begin to pull me out of the clubs and into a completely different future.

1999: Diane Pearce and the Prophetic Encounter

In 1999, still very much in the club world, I went to a meeting at Hillview Community Church in Rowville. Prophet Diane Pearce was ministering that night, at 'Aussie John' and Pauline Arnott's church.

I didn't go looking for a life-changing encounter. I went because a friend told me about her connection to God and because, deep down, I was hungry, even if I wouldn't have admitted it.

During worship, something began to happen.

The presence of God filled the room in a way I couldn't ignore. It wasn't hype. It wasn't emotional manipulation. It was weighty, tender, holy. I felt like the air grew thicker.

Without really knowing why, I started to weep.

Not polite tears, deep, heaving sobs. Years of pain, shame, and exhaustion started to surface. I couldn't hold it together anymore, and honestly, I didn't want to.

As I wiped my eyes, I realised everyone had left the meeting, the live worship had moved to a CD and there was only Diane at the front of the room pacing slowly back and forth, and John and Pauline sitting quietly in the corner.

I thought it was my time to leave, but as I stood up, my legs had a different idea, and literally walked me to the front where Diane was, this was something I had never experienced before.

Diane walked over to me. She looked at me with such kindness and said,"I've been waiting for you."

Those words went straight past my defences and into my heart. I didn't even know this woman, but it felt like God Himself was saying, "I see you. I've been waiting for this moment."

For about twenty-five minutes, she prophesied over me.

She spoke life, restoration, healing, and destiny. She called out things in me that no one else knew, wounds I'd never voiced, desires I'd buried, parts of me that had never had language or validation. It was as if God was reading my internal journal out loud, but with love, not exposure.

She didn't focus on my sin. She focused on my calling.
She didn't rehearse my failures. She named my future.

Something in me that had been slumbering for a long time started to awaken.

When she finished, Aussie John Arnott stepped forward and said something I'll never forget:

"Can I give you a hug?"

I thought this was weird, but it couldn't get any weirder than what I had already experienced.

So, I said yes.

He wrapped his arms around me and held me, not briefly, not awkwardly, but with the steady, safe embrace of a father.

He then said, "Lawrence I want to give you this big daddy hug"

In that hug, something shifted.

For the first time in my life, I felt what it was like to be held by a father:

- Not with conditions.
- Not with expectations.
- Not with performance attached.

Just love.

I cried into his chest like a little boy. Years of father hunger surfaced in that embrace. It wasn't just John holding me; it was as if the Father Himself was saying, "This is what you were made for. This is the kind of love you were always meant to know."

That night marked me.

I still went back to the clubs. I still performed. I still wrestled with my old patterns.

But something had changed.

A seed had been planted, a prophetic picture of who I really was and where God was taking me. And once you've tasted that, the old life never quite satisfies in the same way again.

John and Pauline Arnott: Twelve Years of Unconditional Love

After that encounter, John and his wife Pauline became spiritual parents to me.

For the next twelve years, they loved me with a kind of steady, unhurried, unconditional love I had never experienced before.

They knew my story. They knew I was still in the clubs. They knew I was still performing as MizDomina and later with drugs. They knew I was far from 'sorted.'

And they loved me anyway.

They didn't sit me down for regular correction sessions. They didn't threaten to withdraw their relationship if I didn't change fast enough. They didn't use shame or fear to try to control me.

They simply stayed.

They listened. They prayed. They checked in. They celebrated small steps. They reminded me of who I was when I forgot. They created a relational space where I could be honest without fear of being cut off.

I kept waiting for the axe to fall.

I expected the conversation to come:

"Lawrence, it's been eight years now. When are you going to get your act together?"
"We love you, but we can't keep walking with you if you're still in that lifestyle."

But it never came.

Instead, what came — again and again — was love.

Not permissive love that says, "Do whatever you want, it doesn't matter."

Holy love that says, "You matter so much that we're not going anywhere."

Their patience gave me a living picture of the Father's heart:

- Not impatient.
- Not condemning.
- Not demanding instant change.

But present. Kind. Steadfast.

That kind of love changes you.

Melbourne Cup 2010: The Deliverance

By 2010, something had been shifting inside me for a while. The clubs were losing their shine. The persona felt... heavier to carry. The gap between who I was on stage and who I was with God was becoming unbearable.

That year, Over the Melbourne Cup weekend a big horse-racing event, and lots of partying in the clubs. It was not a 'holy' environment by any stretch. It was loud, crowded, full of alcohol, drugs, and the usual chaos.

But God doesn't wait for church services to move.

Somewhere in the middle of that day, I had a powerful encounter with the Holy Spirit. There was no worship band, no altar call, no prayer line. Just a God and me in the middle-of-the-day party.

It's hard to put into words, but it felt like something inside me snapped, in a good way.

Lies I'd believed for years started to come to the surface:

- "You'll always be this way."
- "This is all you're good for."
- "You're too far gone to change now."

In that moment, it was as if the Holy Spirit said, "Enough."

I felt a deep internal shift, like chains loosening, like a weight lifting off my chest. Tears came again, uninvited. I knew, standing there in that middle-of-the-day party, that something of the enemy's hold on my life had been broken.

It wasn't dramatic in the way some deliverance stories are told, no shouting, no rolling on the floor. But it was real.

And it marked the beginning of the end of my time in the clubs.

From that point on, the grace to stay in that world lifted. What I had once loved, even enjoyed, became awful. The dissonance between who God said I was and how I was living became too loud to ignore.

Within a short time, I stepped out of the club scene for good.

The Patience of God

Looking back on those twelve years, from Travis' invitation, to Diane's prophetic word, to John and Pauline's steady love, to that quiet deliverance at the Melbourne Cup day party, I'm overwhelmed by the patience of God.

Twelve years.

Twelve years of walking with me in the mess.
Twelve years of loving me while I was still running.
Twelve years of sending people, words, and encounters at just the right time.
Twelve years of waiting for the moment when I would finally be ready to receive what He'd been offering all along.

That's the Father's heart.

Not impatient. Not condemning. Not standing at a distance with arms crossed, tapping His foot, saying, "Hurry up."

Patient. Kind. Loving.

He's not in a rush to fix you so you can be useful.

He's committed to walking with you so you can be whole.

He waited for the day when His love would finally break through every wall I'd built, and He'll do the same for you.

HEART WORK

Reflection, Prayer, and Encounter

Scripture

"God is sheer mercy and grace; not easily angered, he's rich in love. He doesn't endlessly nag and scold, nor hold grudges forever."

— Psalm 103:8–9 (The Message)

Reflection Questions

Choose 1-3 questions that stand out to you today. You don't need to answer them all.

If you're reading in a group, you may choose one question to share and keep the rest private.

- Where have you experienced God's patience in your life? How long has He been waiting for you?

- Have you ever felt like you were 'doing Christianity wrong' because transformation wasn't happening fast enough?

- Who in your life has loved you unconditionally, without rushing to correct or fix you?

- Are you waiting for 'the axe to fall' in any relationship with God or with people?

- What would it look like to see the process itself as part of God's goodness, rather than demanding instant change?

Journal Prompt

"The part of my journey that has taken the longest is… and I've believed that means…"

Write honestly about the slow places, the stuck places, the "why is this taking so long?" places. Then ask the Father, "What are You doing in the waiting?"

Your Reflections:

One Thing to Try This Week

Look back over the last year (or five, or ten). Write down one way you've changed, even a small one that you didn't orchestrate yourself. Thank God for His patient, persistent work in you.

Breath Prayer for This Week

Inhale: "You are patient with me"
Exhale: "You don't give up"

Let this truth quiet the voice that says you're taking too long.

Soaking Exercise

Resting in the Long Journey

1. Find a quiet space and invite the Holy Spirit to meet you.
2. Close your eyes and take a few deep breaths. Let your body relax.
3. Picture yourself on a long road. You've been walking for a while. You're tired.
4. Now notice: Jesus is walking beside you. He's not rushing you. He's not frustrated.
5. Ask Him, "How do You feel about how long this is taking?"
6. Wait. Listen. Notice His face, His tone, His posture toward you.
7. Ask Him, "What are You doing in me during this long season?"
8. Rest in whatever He shows you. Let Him carry the pressure you've been holding.

What did you notice?

Prayer

Father,
I confess I've been frustrated with how long this is taking.
I've compared my journey to others.
I've wondered if I'm doing something wrong,
if You've given up on me,
or if transformation will ever really come.

Thank You for Your patience.
Thank You that You don't nag, scold, or hold grudges.
Thank You that You're not in a hurry with me.

Help me to trust the process,
the slow work, the hidden seasons, the long obedience.

May I learn to see Your goodness not just in the breakthroughs,
but in the waiting, the wrestling, and the small steps forward.

I'm still on the journey.
And You're still with me.

Amen.

PART II

ENCOUNTERING THE FATHER'S HEART

PREFACE

A gentle note: for some readers, the word 'Father' may feel tender or complicated especially if your story includes harm from a father figure or spiritual authority. Please go slowly. You don't have to force language that doesn't feel safe. My anchor is simple: if you want to know what the Father is like, look at Jesus.

If Part I is the story of hunger and wounding, Part II is the story of what happens when God meets us inside that hunger.

I used to think healing would come through effort, through trying harder, doing better, being more spiritual, more disciplined, more 'together.' But the turning point in my life didn't begin with my strength. It began with an encounter: the Father drawing near, not with disappointment, but with kindness.

Part II traces the slow, sometimes surprising movement from orphan-hearted striving into beloved identity. It's not a straight line. It's not a 'before and after' that ties everything up neatly. It's more like learning a new language, learning to receive love, to trust presence, to recognise God's voice as gentle rather than demanding.

In these chapters I share some of the moments and revelations that reshaped my inner world: learning to receive, discovering the Father's heart, and noticing how even good ministry can become 'prophetic leaking' when it flows from need rather than fullness.

If you're reading this and you feel tired, ashamed, stuck, or spiritually numb, I want to offer you hope: God is not waiting for you to get it all right before He comes close. The Father's love is not fragile. It does not withdraw when you're in process.

As you read Part II, my invitation is simple: don't rush. Let the story create space for your own story. And if you find yourself longing — longing for safety, for belonging, for a love that stays — pay attention to that longing. It may be the beginning of an encounter for you, too.

CHAPTER 5

THE FATHER'S LOVE

Everything changed in January 2011.

Not because I finally got my act together.
Not because I cleaned myself up.
Not because I earned anything.

Everything changed because I became aware of the Father who was always there.

Leaders School of Ministry: January 2011

In January 2011, I attended an **International Leaders School of Ministry** (ILSOM) in my home town of Melbourne, Australia, hosted by John and Pauline Arnott, with John and Carol Arnott, and Alyn & AJ Jones. The atmosphere was thick with the presence of God — familiar, but different.

I'd been to conferences before. I'd experienced powerful worship, solid teaching, and prayer ministry. But this wasn't just another event.

This was an awakening encounter.

"The Father Loves You Just as Much as He Loves Jesus"

During one of the sessions, someone read John 17:23:

"I in them and You in Me — so that they may be brought to complete unity. Then the world will know that You sent Me and have loved them even as You have loved Me."

Then they said a sentence that stopped me in my tracks:

"The Father loves you just as much as He loves Jesus."

I'd heard that before. Theologically, I knew it was in the Bible. I could have preached it to someone else.

But I had never experienced or awakened to it.

At that moment, something inside me cracked open.

The Encounter that Awakened me

I began to weep. Not polite tears, but deep, guttural sobs that came from places I didn't even know were still alive.

And then I felt it.

The Father's arms around me.

Not metaphorically. Not as a nice image for a sermon.

I felt Him holding me. Embracing me. Loving me.

And in that embrace, I heard Him say:

"Lawrence, I love you just the same amount that I love Jesus."

Not less.
Not conditionally.
Not 'one day, when you've finally cleaned up.'

The same amount.

The same love He has for His perfect Son, He has for me. His broken, messy, wounded son.

Something in me that had been braced for rejection my whole life finally exhaled.

Deliverance in the Father's Arms

As the Father held me, freedom began to happen. Carol Arnott came over, laid hands on me, and prayed as I lay on the floor — soaking in a deep impartation of the Father's love.

Lies started breaking off. Chains started loosening. Walls started crumbling.

- The lie that I wasn't wanted.
- The lie that I wasn't enough.
- The lie that I had to perform to be loved.
- The lie that God was always slightly disappointed with me.

All of it, breaking.

And in their place, the Father was speaking truth:

"You are Mine.
You are loved.
You are wanted.
You belong."

It wasn't a deliverance session with shouting and drama. It was deliverance by embrace. The Father's love was doing what no amount of striving, self-hatred, or religious effort could do.

The Wound Beneath All the Wounds

In that moment, I realised something profound:

The father wound was at the root of everything that caused the illusion of separation in my heart.

The abuse, the addiction, the drag persona, the club scene, the desperate search for identity and belonging — so much of it had grown in the vacuum left by a father's absence, and the lies that took root there.

When the Father showed up and filled that void, everything else began to shift.

Not instantly. Not all at once. But the root had been touched.

And when you heal the root, the fruit in your life begins to change.

I Am My Father's Son

After that awakening encounter, my identity shifted.

I no longer walked with orphan tendencies, endlessly searching for a place to belong.
I no longer performed, trying to earn love through perfection, ministry, or spiritual intensity.

I was a son.

A son of the Father, loved, wanted, valued, cherished.

Not because of what I did, but because of who He is.

And that changed everything.

When the Father Reintroduces Himself

Years later, as I was still processing what had happened to me at the **School of Ministry,** my friend Dubb shared a question that put words to my experience. It wasn't a clever line; it was a mirror.

"What if the Father needs to reintroduce Himself to you? What if you've believed Jesus came to save you from Him?"

When I read that, I wept — because it named the fear I'd been living under.

For years, I had absorbed a picture of God where the Father felt angry and unsafe, and Jesus felt like the only place I could hide. I didn't always say it out loud, but it was there underneath everything: the sense that God's holiness meant distance, that God's disappointment was the default, and that love had to be earned.

So I clung to Jesus because Jesus felt kind. Jesus felt approachable. Jesus felt like He actually wanted me. But the Father? The Father felt like the One I had to be careful around — like one wrong move and I'd be exposed, rejected, or punished.

I'm not trying to pick a fight with anyone's theology on Penal Substitutionary Atonement[1] here — I'm simply telling the truth about what that picture did inside me. It didn't make me love God more. It made me hide. It made me perform. It made me relate to God like an orphan — always braced, always striving, always waiting for the other shoe to drop.

And then the Father met me.

Not as the distant God I'd been taught to fear, but as the Father revealed in Jesus — close, present, and full of mercy. The One who runs toward prodigals.

'Prodigal' means one who spends or gives lavishly; recklessly and wastefully extravagant.

---

[1] Christians hold a range of views on the atonement. I'm sharing the framework that brought healing to my own relationship with God and helped me encounter the Father's love as revealed in Jesus.

So in fact, the 'prodigal' was not the son, but the Father — the One who offered reckless, extravagant grace, forgiveness, and intimacy to his sons then, and to us, his children now!

He is the One who touches the unclean. The One who doesn't flinch at broken people, but moves toward them.

That question sent me on a journey toward what many call the **Christus Victor** emphasis: Jesus defeating sin, death, and the powers of darkness, and bringing us home as beloved children. Not a transaction to convince the Father to love us, but a rescue that reveals the Father's love has been there all along.

A rescue.
A healing.
A homecoming.

Because that's exactly what I had believed — and that's what the Father was healing in me.

The Lie I Lived Under

For years, I thought Jesus came to save me from the Father.

I thought the Father was angry, disappointed, and distant, holy in a way that meant He couldn't stand the sight of me. In my mind, Jesus was the kind, loving one who stepped in to take the hit so the Father wouldn't destroy me.

That's what I'd been taught. That's what I'd absorbed from sermons, songs, and Christian culture.

And that belief shaped everything:

- how I saw God;
- how I saw myself; and
- how I approached prayer, worship, and ministry.

I was terrified of the Father.

So, I clung to Jesus, because Jesus felt safe. Jesus felt kind. Jesus felt like He actually liked me.

But the Father? The Father felt dangerous.

But that's not the truth.

The Truth: Jesus Reveals the Father

The Father has always been as Jesus was when He walked the earth, and as the Holy Spirit is now.

The Father isn't the angry one that Jesus has to protect you from. He's not waiting with crossed arms, keeping score, holding back affection until you 'get it right'

He's good. He has always been good.

Jesus didn't come to save you from the Father.
Jesus came to reveal the Father.

To show you what He's always been like. To reintroduce you to the One you've been running from. To rescue you from the lies you've believed, and from the system of darkness that told you God was angry and you had to earn His love.

That's the Christus Victor emphasis: not Jesus taking a beating from an enraged Father, but Jesus defeating sin, death, and the powers of darkness — dismantling the lies, breaking the grip of shame, and opening the way into new life.

A rescue.
A healing.
A homecoming.

That's what happened to me at the **Catch The Fire School of Ministry**.

The Father reintroduced Himself.

Not as the angry, distant, disappointed God I'd been taught about, but as the loving, present, delighted Father He'd always been.

When He said, "Lawrence, I love you the same amount that I love Jesus," He was saying:

"I'm not who you think I am. Let Me show you who I really am."

"God Was in Christ…"

The apostle Paul says it this way in 2 Corinthians 5:19:

"God was in Christ reconciling the world to Himself, not counting their trespasses against them."

Read that again slowly.

God was **in** Christ.
Not standing at a distance, watching Jesus take the hit.
In Christ, reconciling the world to Himself.

And He was **not** counting their trespasses against them.

He wasn't keeping a list. He wasn't waiting to punish. He wasn't turning His face away in disgust.

He was bringing us home.

"God Can't Look Upon Sin"?

Another lie that kept me hiding, ashamed, and afraid to come to the Father was this line I heard over and over:

"God can't look upon sin."

It sounded biblical. It seemed to fit my image of a holy God who couldn't bear to be near someone like me. I was told that's why Jesus had to die, so the Father could finally stand to look at me.

But that's not the full story.

A revivalist and teacher, Chris Gore, expresses it this way:

"The notion that 'God can't look upon sin' can be misunderstood if it suggests God is distant or repulsed by us. Rather, through Jesus, we see God entering our brokenness to draw people close, that they would encounter the love of a Father. It's not about God turning away, but about His unwavering commitment to mend what's shattered."

Jesus, the fullness of God, immersed Himself in humanity's mess — sharing meals with tax collectors, touching lepers, and connecting with those labelled as 'sinners'. The world doesn't need punishment; it craves and needs healing.

This incorrect notion often stems from Habakkuk 1:13, when the prophet says, "Your eyes are too pure to behold/look upon sin." But the very next verse goes on to say, "So why do You?"

Let That Sink In

God never turned away.

Not when Adam and Eve sinned.
Not when Israel rebelled.
Not when I was in the clubs, performing as MizDomina, high and hiding.

He never turned away.

Instead, He entered the mess.

Jesus, the fullness of God, immersed Himself in all humanity's brokenness. He shared meals with drug dealers. He touched prostitutes. He drew near to those labelled 'faggots.'

He didn't turn away. He moved toward.

If Jesus is what God looks like, then God is not the One who can't bear to look at you. He's the One who comes looking for you.

Habakkuk 1:13 — A Misunderstood Cry

The verse often quoted to support 'God can't look upon sin' is Habakkuk 1:13:

"Your eyes are too pure to look on evil; You cannot tolerate wrongdoing."

But most people stop there.

The very next line says:

"So why do You?"

Habakkuk isn't writing a neat doctrinal statement about God's inability to be near sin. He's crying out in confusion:

"If You're so holy, why are You letting this happen? Why aren't You doing something?"

It's a lament, not a systematic theology.

We've taken a line from a prophet's wrestle and turned it into a doctrine that keeps people hiding from the very God who came to heal them.

The God revealed in Jesus does not stand far off from sin. He walks straight into the middle of it to rescue the people trapped there.

Jesus: The Fullness of God

Colossians 2:9 says:

"For in Christ all the fullness of the Deity lives in bodily form."

All the fullness of God. In Jesus.

And what did Jesus do?

He touched lepers.
He ate with 'sinners'.
He defended the woman caught in adultery.
He restored Peter after betrayal.
He told stories about a Father running down the road to embrace a son who smelled like pigs and bad decisions.

He never turned away.

If you want to know what the Father is like, look at Jesus.

Not distant. Not repulsed. Not unable to look upon you.

But entering your brokenness to draw you close.

The Father in the Nightclubs

That's what I experienced during those twelve years in the clubs.

I thought God had left. I thought He was disgusted. I thought He couldn't even look at me.

But He was there.

The whole time.

Not condemning. Not shaming. Not turning away.

Drawing close. Whispering truth. Waiting for the moment I'd finally be able to receive what He'd been offering all along: His unwavering commitment to mend what was shattered.

Chris Gore is right: "The world doesn't need punishment; it craves and needs healing."

That's what I needed.

Not punishment.
Not a lecture.
Not a divine "I told you so."

I needed healing.

And the Father knew that.

So, He didn't turn away. He didn't wait for me to clean up. He didn't keep His distance until I was 'worthy.'

He entered my brokenness to draw me close.

And when I finally encountered Him at the **School of Ministry** in 2011, I realised:

He'd been there all along.

The Father You've Been Looking For

If you've been running from the Father; if you've believed He's angry, distant, or disappointed; I want to invite you to let Him reintroduce Himself.

Not as the God you've been taught to fear, but as the God revealed in Jesus.

The Father who loves you just as much as He loves Jesus.
The Father who has never turned away, even in your darkest moments.
The Father who entered your mess to bring you home.

That's who He is.
That's who He's always been.

And He's waiting for you.

With open arms.
With a smile on His face.
With joy in His heart.

Come home.

HEART WORK

Reflection, Prayer, and Encounter

Scripture

"Look with wonder at the depth of the Father's marvelous love that he has lavished on us! He has called us and made us his very own beloved children."

— 1 John 3:1a (TPT)

"Consider the incredible love the Father has given us — that we should be called children of God, and that is exactly what we are!"

— 1 John 3:1 (The Remedy)

Reflection Questions

Choose 1-3 questions that stand out to you today. You don't need to answer them all.

If you're reading in a group, you may choose one question to share and keep the rest private.

- What lies have you believed about God the Father because of your earthly father or other authority figures?
- Can you imagine the Father loving you as much as He loves Jesus? What makes that hard to believe?
- Where do you need the Father to show up and heal the father wound in your heart?
- Have you believed the lie that 'God can't look upon sin?' How has that shaped your relationship with Him?

- What would it look like to let the Father reintroduce Himself to you?

Journal Prompt

"When I think of God as Father, I feel… because…"

Be honest. If it's fear, distance, or confusion — write it. Then ask Him, "Father, who are You really? Show me Your true heart toward me."

Your Reflections:

One Thing to Try This Week

Sit quietly and ask the Father, "How do You feel about me right now — in this moment, as I am?" Write down the first thing that comes to mind, even if it surprises you.

Breath Prayer for This Week

Inhale: "I am Your beloved"
Exhale: "You delight in me"

Let this truth replace the lies you've believed about His heart toward you.

Soaking Exercise
Meeting the Father's True Face

1. Find a quiet, safe space. Invite the Holy Spirit to guide you gently.
2. Close your eyes and take a few deep breaths. Let yourself settle.
3. Picture yourself standing before the Father. Notice how you feel, nervous, distant, afraid, curious?
4. Ask Him, "Father, what is Your face like when You look at me?"
5. Wait. Let Him show you. Notice His expression, His eyes, His posture.
6. If fear or shame rises, don't push it away. Just notice it, and ask Him, "What do You want to say to this fear?"
7. Rest in His presence. Let Him reintroduce Himself to you — not as the father you've known, but as He truly is.

What did you notice?

Prayer

Father,
I've carried so many lies about who You are.
I've projected my earthly father's face onto Yours.
I've believed You were distant, disappointed, or angry.

Forgive me for the ways I've misunderstood Your heart.

I invite You to reintroduce Yourself to me.
Show me Your true face —
the One who runs toward me,
the One who delights in me,
the One who has never turned away.

Heal the father wound in my heart.
May I learn what it means to be loved by You,
not because I've earned it,
but because I am Yours.

I receive Your love today.
I am Your beloved child.

Let it be so.

Amen.

LEARNING TO RECEIVE

After my awakening encounter with the Father at the **Catch The Fire School of Ministry**, something shifted.

I knew I was loved.
I knew I was His son.

But I quickly discovered that knowing you're loved in your head and actually receiving that love in your heart are two very different things.

I had a new identity, but old habits, especially around striving and performance, don't disappear overnight.

The Door in My Heart

During one of my early soaking times after the **School of Ministry**, I had a simple but powerful vision.

I saw a door.

On the other side of the door was the Father, standing there with a gift in His hands. I somehow knew what the gift was:

His love.
His acceptance.
His delight in me.

He wasn't hiding. He wasn't pacing impatiently. He was just there, calm, kind, waiting.

But in the vision, I was standing on my side of the door, hand on the handle, frozen.

I wasn't locked out.
He wasn't refusing to open up.

I was afraid to open the door. Why?

This was the door I had locked years earlier to keep my heart safe. Yet, it is also the same door that let's love in.

Afraid yes, not because the Father was withholding, but because I didn't know what to do with a love I didn't have to earn.

I'd spent my whole life performing, striving, and proving:

- If I did well, I might be tolerated.
- If I excelled, I might be accepted.
- If I was impressive enough, I might be loved.

And now the Father was offering me something I couldn't work for.

All I had to do was receive.

But I didn't know how.

Connie Sinnott's Hug

A few years later, **Catch the Fire** hosted an event in Melbourne with Connie and Jeremy Sinnott who came from Canada. Connie had become a spiritual mother, one of those people who carries the Father's love in a way you can feel it in the room.

After one of the sessions, we were chatting and she said, very simply:

"Lawrence, can I give you a hug?"

I said yes.

She stepped in and wrapped her arms around me. From the outside, it probably looked like a normal hug. But inside, I was stiff as a board, awkward, guarded, unable to relax.

I didn't even realise how tense I was until she gently pulled back, looked me straight in the eyes, and said, "Lawrence, you don't know how to receive, do you?"

Something in me broke.

Tears welled up. The question went straight to the core of that door vision in my heart. She had named what I couldn't articulate.

I didn't know how to receive.

I knew how to serve.
I knew how to minister.
I knew how to perform and care and pour out.

But to simply stand there and let love come toward me without earning it? That felt terrifying.

Connie smiled, no shame, no frustration and said, "Let's try this again."

She drew me into another hug. This time, I made a choice: to let go. To soften. To stop holding myself together and allow myself to be held.

As she embraced me, I felt something like a mother's embrace, a different expression to my earthy mother's embrace, something deeper I've never really known, nurturing, life-giving, safe. It was as if the Father was saying, through her arms, "You don't have to be 'on' right now. You can just be."

I wept into her shoulder, and a new kind of receiving began.

Soaking in "I Love You"

After that, I felt the invitation of the Father,

"Every time you soak, I want you to just let me say, I love you. That's it. Don't ask for anything. Don't intercede for anyone. Don't try to get a word for someone else. Just receive My love."

That sounded both beautiful and deeply uncomfortable.

But I knew it was an invitation.

So, I did it.

For the next six months, I set aside time every day to soak in God's presence and do nothing but let the Father say, "I love you."

No prayer list.
No ministry agenda.
No trying to 'be productive' spiritually.

Just lying there, letting love wash over me.

At first, it felt awkward. I kept wanting to jump up and do something, pray for others, make declarations, be 'useful.' Part of me felt like I was wasting time.

But slowly, something began to shift.

The words, "I love you." started to move from theory to reality. They weren't just a verse on a page; they were a voice in my heart.

I began to believe it, not just in my head, but in the places that had been braced for rejection my whole life.

I began to receive.

Learning to Receive, Not Just Give

My whole life, I'd been a provider.

I gave love, attention, care, and ministry. I poured out for others in church, in friendships, in leadership. On the outside, it looked generous and spiritual.

On the inside, I was running on fumes.

Here's the truth I had to face:

You can't give what you don't have.

If you're constantly pouring out without being filled up, you will eventually run dry. And when you're empty, ministry becomes performance, relationships become draining, and 'serving' becomes a way to avoid your own pain.

That's where I was.

I was ministering to others, but I was empty inside. I was telling people about the Father's love, but I wasn't letting that love land in my own heart.

The Father wasn't impressed by my capacity to give. He was inviting me to stop, to rest, and to receive.

To let Him fill me up.

What Is Soaking?

Soaking became one of the main ways I learned to receive.

Soaking is simply resting in the presence of God.

It's not intercession.
It's not worship in the usual 'sing loud and push through' sense.
It's not Bible study or teaching prep.

It's just being with Him.

No agenda.
No performance.
No striving.

Just receiving.

How to Soak (A Practical Guide)

Here's how I soak. You can adapt this to your own personality and season:

1. **Find a quiet space.**

   Somewhere you won't be interrupted, your bedroom, a corner of the lounge, even your car in a quiet spot.

2. **Put on soaking music.**

   Instrumental worship, gentle worship songs, or even silence, whatever helps you rest rather than analyse.

3. **Get comfortable.**

   Lie down or sit in a relaxed position. This is not about staying 'on duty'; it's about choosing to rest.

4. **Invite the Holy Spirit.**

   Pray something simple like, "Holy Spirit, I know you are here, let me become more aware of your Presence that is already here right now, come and fill this space."

5. **Let go of the agenda.**

   You're not here to solve problems, get a strategy, or earn brownie points. You're here to receive.

6. **Rest in His presence.**

   If thoughts come, acknowledge them and let them drift past like clouds. If emotion surfaces, let it. If nothing seems to happen, that's okay, you're still with Him.

7. Receive His love.

Let the Father say, "I love you." Over and over. Picture His arms around you. Let Him hold you. Let Him fill your being.

That's it.

It's simple. But it's deeply transformative.

The Gift of Receiving

Learning to receive has been one of the most important lessons of my healing journey.

Because when you learn to receive, everything changes:

- You stop performing and start resting.
- You stop striving and start trusting.
- You stop trying to earn what has already been given.

You become full.

Full of the Father's love.
Full of His presence.
Full of His peace.

And when you're full, you can pour out without running dry. Ministry becomes overflow instead of obligation. Love becomes a response instead of a performance.

That's the gift of receiving.

HEART WORK

Reflection, Prayer, and Encounter

Scripture

"Are you weary, carrying a heavy burden? Come to me. I will refresh your life, for I am your oasis. Simply join your life with mine. Learn my ways and you'll discover that I'm gentle, humble, easy to please. You will find refreshment and rest in me."

— Matthew 11:28–29 (TPT)

Reflection Questions

Choose 1-3 questions that stand out to you today. You don't need to answer them all.

If you're reading in a group, you may choose one question to share and keep the rest private.

- Do you know how to receive love, or do you mostly know how to give it?

- What makes it hard for you to receive from God or from others? Where does that resistance come from?

- Have you ever felt like you were "wasting time" by just resting in God's presence?

- What might it look like for you to practise soaking in God's love in the next season?

- Are you running on empty, constantly giving but rarely being filled? What needs to change?

Journal Prompt

"When someone tries to love me or care for me, I feel... because I believe..."

Write honestly about your resistance to receiving. Then ask the Father, "What would it look like for me to simply rest and let You love me?"

Your Reflections:

____

____

____

____

____

____

____

____

____

One Thing to Try This Week

Set a timer for 10 minutes. Sit or lie down comfortably. Put on instrumental worship music (or silence). Do nothing but receive. Don't pray, don't intercede, don't ask for anything — just be loved.

____

Breath Prayer for This Week

Inhale: "I receive Your love"
Exhale: "I don't have to earn it"

Let this truth quiet the striving and the performing.

Soaking Exercise

Practising the Art of Receiving

1. Find a comfortable place to sit or lie down. Put on gentle instrumental worship music or sit in silence.

2. Close your eyes and take a few deep breaths. Let your body relax.

3. Imagine yourself in a safe, beautiful place — a garden, a quiet room, beside still waters.

4. Jesus is there with you. He's not asking anything of you. He's simply present.

5. Notice how it feels to just be with Him — no agenda, no performance, no words.

6. If your mind wanders or you feel restless, gently bring your attention back to His presence.

7. Ask Him, "What do You want to give me right now?" Then simply receive — peace, love, rest, or just His nearness.

8. Stay as long as you like. When you're ready, thank Him for being your oasis.

What did you notice?

Prayer

Father,
I confess I'm better at doing than receiving.
I'm more comfortable giving than being filled.
I've believed that rest is laziness,
that soaking is wasting time,
that I have to earn Your love by staying busy.

Forgive me for the ways I've resisted Your love.

May I learn to receive.
May I learn to rest in Your presence without an agenda.
May I learn that being loved by You is not passive —
it's the most active, life-giving thing I can do.

Fill me from the overflow of Your heart.
Let me learn to live from belovedness, not for it.

I open my hands, my heart, and my life to You.
I receive Your love today.

Let it be so,

Amen.

FROM ORPHAN TO SON

There are four levels of identity I've discovered on this journey:

Orphan. Son. King. Father.

I first encountered identity and the message of sonship language through John and Carol Arnott at **Catch The Fire**, who had received it from Jack Frost and Jack Winter.

Over the years, this language expanded as my friend Dubb Alexander unpacks in his book *Kingdom Theology, Volume 1: The Kingdom.* I've shared some thoughts on this framework, illustrated within my own story, because it so accurately describes the journey the Father has taken me on.

The movement from one to the next is the journey of transformation, not into a more 'important' Christian, but into deeper maturity in love.

Four Levels of Kingdom Identity

1. Orphan (Tendencies)

An orphan operates from a mindset of scarcity, fear, and performance.

- "I have to earn love."
- "I'm on my own."

- "God is a master, not a Father."
- "I have to strive to survive."

For most of my life, I operated as a son with orphan tendencies as I didn't know who I was.

Even after I became a Christian, even after I encountered Jesus, I still had an orphan mindset. I believed I had to earn God's love. I believed I was on my own. I believed I had to perform to be accepted.

That's the orphan heart.

And it's exhausting.

As I discovered language, it helped me see what I'd been living:

- The root mindset of an orphan is **fear**.
- The native language is **lies**.
- The emotional state is **foreboding** (something bad is coming).
- The primary focus is **survival**.
- The evident characteristic is **insecurity**.
- The manifestation is **sin**, self-protection, self-medication, and self-promotion.

2. Son/Daughter

A son or daughter operates from a mindset of belovedness, rest, and identity.

- "I am loved for who I am, not what I do."
- "I belong to the Father."
- "God is my loving Father."
- "I can rest in His love."

When I encountered the Father at the **Catch The Fire School of Ministry**, I shifted from orphan to son.

I realised I was loved for who I am, not what I do.
I realised I belonged to the Father.
I realised I could rest in His love.

That's the son heart.

And it's liberating.

In sonship:

- The root mindset is **love**.
- The native language is **truth**.
- The emotional state is **peace**.
- The primary focus is **relationship**.
- The evident characteristic is **inner strength**.
- The manifestation is **joy**.

The shift from orphan to son doesn't happen overnight. It's a journey, a process, a daily choice.

Every day, I have to choose: Will I operate with an orphan mindset, or as a son?

Will I strive, or will I rest?
Will I perform, or will I receive?

That's the shift.

3. King/Queen (Kingdom Son/Daughter)

But the journey doesn't stop at sonship.

The Father is inviting us into kingship — what I often call **kingdom sonship** — a place where we not only know we're loved, but we also walk in the authority and inheritance that comes with being His children.

We're not just recipients of His love; we're co-heirs with Christ. We're not just resting in His presence; we're partnering with Him to bring heaven to earth.

A king or queen operates from a mindset of authority, inheritance, and partnership with the Father.

- "I am a co-heir with Christ."
- "I carry real authority in the kingdom."
- "I partner with the Father to bring heaven to earth."
- "I walk in the fullness of my identity and calling."

In kingship:

- The root mindset is **leadership**.
- The native language is **strategy**.
- The emotional state is **confidence** (not arrogance).
- The primary focus is **impact**.
- The evident characteristic is **authority**.
- The manifestation is **solutions**.

One of the biggest shifts in my journey was moving from performance to partnership.

As an orphan, I performed for God's approval.
As a son, I rested in His love.
As a king, I began to partner with Him in His mission.

Not performing. Not striving.

Partnering.

4. Father/Mother

And there is still more.

The highest expression of kingdom identity is **fatherhood and motherhood**, becoming spiritual fathers and mothers who use everything we've received to raise others into their identity and calling.

A father or mother operates from a mindset of inheritance and legacy.

- "What I carry is not just for me; it's for sons and daughters."
- "My ceiling is meant to become their floor."
- "I speak the language of identity and empowerment."
- "I want to leave a trail of sons and daughters who know who they are."

In fatherhood/motherhood:

- The root mindset is **inheritance**.
- The native language is **identity**.
- The emotional state is **compassion**.
- The primary focus is **sons and daughters**.
- The evident characteristic is **empowerment**.
- The manifestation is **legacy**.

When I look at people like John and Pauline Arnott in my life, that's what I see: not just leaders, but spiritual parents.

Orphan Tendencies

Over the years, in prayer ministry sessions and pastoral conversations, I've come to see the orphan–to–sonship journey in a deeper way.

People often talk about 'the spirit of an orphan.' I don't think we need to be 'delivered' from an orphan spirit in the way we sometimes imagine.

But I do believe many of us carry **orphan tendencies**.

We are sons and daughters of our heavenly Father. Our original design was always to be His children. But when delusion entered, when the idea of separation took root, we began to build and perceive life through our wounds, our experiences, and our feelings.

So, what we call a 'spirit of orphanhood' often looks like the ingrained habits of an orphan heart crying out to be loved.

How Does the Heart Respond?

These are some of the questions I've learned to ask:

- Do I see God as a master, or as a loving Father?
- Am I independent and self-reliant, having to do everything alone to survive, or can I trust and be interdependent with the Triune God?
- Do I live by the love of law, or by the law of love?
- Do I live with security and peace, or with anxiety and fear?
- Do I strive for approval, or do I know I'm accepted for who I am, not what I do?
- How do I see myself, through shame, or through belovedness?
- In peer relationships, is there competition, rivalry, jealousy or humility, unity, and celebration of others?
- Is my vision driven by my own ambitions, or am I learning to see as my Father sees?
- Do I feel I have to fight for everything to survive, or does my sonship release a sense of inheritance in all I do?

My Own Orphan Tendencies

There have been many times where I've responded with orphan tendencies.

Selfish. Self-protective. Self-focused.

And in our world, that often seems acceptable, even wise.

You have to do it yourself.
You have to make it happen.
If you don't, who will?

There's some truth in taking responsibility. But here's what I've learned:

It's meant to be an interdependent collaboration with the Trinity, with humanity, with the world around us.

Canadian John Arnott talks about three concurrent journeys:

1. The inward journey with our own hearts.
2. The upward journey with our relationship with God.
3. The outward journey with humanity.

These journeys are not 'either/or' but all flowing together in unity and harmony.

Just as the Father loves the Son, and the Son loves the Father, and the Spirit loves the Father and the Son — so we are invited into that same dynamic: loving and caring for ourselves, loving God, and loving others.

Dealing with Heart Issues

To love well, we have to deal with these heart issues — these orphan tendencies that keep us self-focused just to survive.

Life experiences shape the 'truth' we believe. But our personal truth isn't always **Truth**. It's often just our perspective, our coping mechanism to survive trauma, loss, grief, abandonment, disappointment, rejection, hatred — things our hearts, minds, and spirits were never created to carry.

So, what do we do?

We disconnect. We go into survival mode. We respond with orphan instincts:

"I need to do whatever it takes to survive."

Into that place, there is an invitation.

The Invitation to Be Fathered

There is an invitation to ask the Spirit, to ask the Father, to **father you again**.

What does it look like to ask God as Father to father you?
What does it look like to know you are safe and secure in His embrace?
What are the small steps you can take today to start to embrace that?

I've tried to satisfy my own needs, to medicate pain and trauma and hurt. It doesn't last. It's temporary. We find ourselves back in the same cycles, facing the same patterns.

Maybe — just maybe — your heavenly Father is the key to unlocking those cycles of repetition, pain, and hurt.

Invite Him into those spaces today.

He's not afraid of how messy it looks. Not at all.

A Personal Moment

I remember preparing for a ministry session, feeling anxious.

What if I don't hear God clearly? What if I let them down? What if I'm not anointed enough today?

I realised I was performing. Striving. Trying to earn God's approval.

I was operating from orphan tendencies.

Then I heard the Father whisper, "Lawrence, you're My son. I'm not grading your performance. I'm enjoying your presence. Just be with Me, and let Me do the work."

That shift — from performing to resting — changed everything.

I stopped trying to be the hero and started partnering with the Hero.
I stopped striving for approval and started resting in acceptance.
I stopped operating as an orphan and started operating as a son.

That's the journey.

Not a one-time shift, but a daily choice. A daily invitation to rest in the Father's love.

The Father's Unchanging Heart

Dubb Alexander shared something, (quoting Brian Zahnd) it offered me a 'metanoia' moment, a fresh perspective on how I see the Father:

"Father did not ever (nor does He need to) change His mind about you! His original intent for you and towards you remained unmoved by the fall.
Jesus' appearance in the world as God was to bring us the ability to change our mind (repent) about God!
Jesus did not go to the cross to change God's mind about you, but rather to change your mind about God!
The crucifixion is not a picture of what God does but rather a picture of Who God is!
Father has always been as Jesus was and Holy Spirit is:
FOR YOU — not against you

CELEBRATING YOU — not tolerating you
ONE WITH YOU — not distant from you."

Let that sink in.

The Father did not change His mind about you.

Not after the fall. Not after your sin. Not after your worst moments.

His original intent for you — His design and purpose — remained unmoved.

God's love is unchanging, but reconciliation is received as we repent (*metanoia* — a change of mind and a turning of the heart) and trust Jesus — because at the cross and resurrection, Jesus truly broke the power of sin and death and opened the way into new life.

The cross wasn't about changing God's mind about you.

The cross was about changing your mind about God.

The Orphan Believes…

The orphan believes God is against them. That God is disappointed. Distant. Barely tolerating them.

The orphan believes they have to earn God's approval, perform to be accepted, prove they're worthy.

The orphan believes the cross was about appeasing an angry God so He could finally love them.

But that's not the truth.

The Son Knows…

The son knows the Father has always been for them.
The son knows the Father is celebrating them, not just tolerating them.

The son knows the Father is one with them, not distant. The son knows the cross wasn't about changing God's mind — it was about revealing God's heart.

A heart that has always been outrageous love.

This Changes Everything

When you realise the Father has never changed His mind about you — that He's always been for you, celebrating you, one with you — everything shifts.

You stop performing and start resting. You stop striving and start receiving. You stop trying to earn what you already have.

That's the shift from orphan to son.

Not because God changed, but because you finally see Him as He's always been.

Where Are You?

So where are you on this kingdom identity journey?

- Are you still operating as an orphan — striving, performing, trying to earn love?
- Are you stepping into sonship — resting, receiving, knowing you're loved?
- Are you beginning to walk as a king or queen — partnering with the Father, carrying solutions and authority?
- Are you starting to step into spiritual fathering or mothering — using what you carry to raise others?

Wherever you are, the Father is inviting you forward.

Not through striving. Not through performance.

Through receiving.

Receiving His love. Receiving your identity. Receiving your inheritance.

And then walking in it.

HEART WORK

Reflection, Prayer, and Encounter

Scripture

"And you did not receive the 'spirit of religious duty,' leading you back into the fear of never being good enough. But you have received the 'Spirit of full acceptance,' enfolding you into the family of God. And you will never feel orphaned, for as he rises up within us, our spirits join him in saying the words of tender affection, 'Beloved Father!'"

— Romans 8:15 (TPT)

You did not receive a spirit of slavery again to fear, but you received the Spirit of sonship, whereby we cry out, 'Abba, Father!'"

— Romans 8:15 (Mirror Bible)

Reflection Questions

Choose 1-3 questions that stand out to you today. You don't need to answer them all.

If you're reading in a group, you may choose one question to share and keep the rest private.

- Do you operate more as an orphan or as a son/daughter? What evidence do you see in your life?

- Which orphan tendencies (striving, comparison, fear of rejection, self-protection) do you recognise in yourself?

- Can you believe that the Father has never changed His mind about you? Why or why not?
- What would it look like for you to shift from performing to resting?
- How would your life change if you fully believed you were a beloved son or daughter?

Journal Prompt

"The orphan voice in my head says... but the Father's voice says..."

Write down the lies the orphan mindset whispers to you. Then ask the Father, "What is the truth? What do You say about me?"

Your Reflections:

One Thing to Try This Week

Notice when you slip into orphan thinking — striving, comparing, or fearing rejection. Pause and say out loud, "I am not an orphan. I am a son/daughter. The Father has never changed His mind about me."

Breath Prayer for This Week

Inhale: "Abba, Father"
Exhale: "I am Yours"

Let this truth settle deeper than the orphan lies.

Soaking Exercise

From Orphan to Beloved

1. Find a quiet space and invite the Holy Spirit to meet you.

2. Close your eyes and take a few deep breaths. Let yourself settle.

3. Picture yourself as an orphan — striving, performing, afraid, alone. Notice how that feels in your body.

4. Now picture the Father approaching you. He's not disappointed. He's not distant.

5. He says, "You are not an orphan. You are My beloved child."

6. Notice what happens in your heart. Do you believe Him? Do you resist? Do you want to, but can't quite?

7. Ask Him, "What would change in my life if I truly believed I was Your son/daughter?"

8. Rest in His presence. Let Him speak identity over you — not based on what you do, but on whose you are.

What did you notice?

Prayer

Father,
I confess I've lived more like an orphan than a son/daughter.
I've strived for approval.
I've compared myself to others.
I've feared rejection and protected my heart.
I've believed I had to earn my place in Your family.

Forgive me for the ways I've forgotten who I am.

Remind me today:
I am not an orphan.
I am Your beloved child.
You have never changed Your mind about me.

May I learn to live from rest, not striving.
May I learn to live from sonship, not performance.
May I learn that my identity is not based on what I do,
but on whose I am.

I am Yours.
And that is enough.

Let it be so.

Amen.

CHAPTER 8

PROPHETIC LEAKING

When you spend time in the Father's presence, something happens.

You get so filled up with His love, you start to leak it everywhere you go.

Not intentionally. Not strategically. But naturally.

You leak what you're soaking in.

If you're soaking in shame, you'll leak shame.
If you're soaking in fear, you'll leak fear.
If you're soaking in the Father's love, you'll leak love.

This is where prophecy really begins — not with a microphone, but with a heart that's been marinated in His presence.

Popcorn Prophetic

I call it 'popcorn prophetic.'

When you're soaking in the Father's love, resting in His presence, receiving His heart, it starts to overflow. It's like kernels sitting in hot oil. Nothing happens for a while, and then suddenly: pop… pop pop pop.

You're in a café and feel a nudge for the barista.
You're at church and see someone in worship and feel a phrase drop into your spirit.
You're on the tram and suddenly sense God's compassion for the person across from you.

You start seeing people the way He sees them.
You start hearing His heart for them.
You start speaking life and destiny over them.

Not because you're trying to be 'prophetic.'

But because you're full.

And what's inside you naturally comes out.

The First Word

My first prophetic activation experience happened at the **Catch The Fire** School in January 2011.

After my encounter with the Father, I was walking through the conference centre and saw a man I'd never met before. He wasn't doing anything dramatic — just standing there, looking a little tired, a little worn.

Suddenly, I heard the Father's voice:

"Tell him I see him.
Tell him I know his name.
Tell him he's not forgotten."

I was terrified.

I didn't know him. I didn't know if I was hearing correctly. I didn't want to look foolish or make something up. Everything in me wanted to walk past and pretend I hadn't heard anything.

But there was a stronger pull inside, the same Presence I'd encountered on the floor the day before.

So, I stepped out in faith.

I walked up to him and said, "Excuse me, I don't know you, but I feel like the Father wants you to know that He sees you. He knows your name. You're not forgotten."

He was overwhelmed.

"I've been feeling invisible for months," he said through emotion. "I've been asking God if He even knows I exist. Thank you."

That was my first prophetic word.

And it wasn't because I was gifted or anointed or special.

It was because I was full of the Father's love.

And it leaked out. That's what prophetic leaking is.

What Prophetic Leaking Really Is

It's not primarily about having a prophetic gift (though some do). It's not about being a prophet (though some are).

It's about being so full of the Father's love that it naturally overflows onto others.

- When you soak in His presence, you start to see people the way He sees them.
- When you rest in His love, you start to hear His heart for them.
- When you receive His truth, you start to speak life over them.

That's prophetic leaking.

And it's available to everyone.

You don't need a title. You need a tender, listening heart.

A Pastoral Disclaimer

Before I share the next story, I need to be absolutely clear:

This is **my personal experience**, not a ministry model.

I do **not** support or offer any form of 'suppression' or 'conversion' practices aimed at changing someone's sexuality. These practices are dangerous, harmful, and often deeply traumatising.

I also want to acknowledge that most gay people do not experience their sexuality as a 'problem' to be fixed. They experience it as part of who they are, often with great honesty and cost. You cannot simply tell someone they are wrong for what they feel or desire and call that love.

Jesus was always moved with compassion. If we are not moved with the same love and compassion, we will hurt people. You can't give away what you haven't received, so perhaps you need to receive more love before you try and deliver 'your' truth.

With that in mind, I offer this story simply as one man's encounter with God in a very complex and tender area of identity.

"Am I Gay?" – A Very Personal Prophetic Story

Be reminded, this was *my* personal discernment journey, and I'm not offering it as a template for anyone else. I reject coercion and conversion therapy in every form. Many faithful Christians hold different convictions and experiences here, and I honour the complexity. What I'm testifying to is this: God met me with love, patience, and truth; and, He will meet you, too.

One of my greatest delights now, in sharing the Father's heart, is speaking destiny, hope, and restoration.

For many years, my sense of identity was shaped by what happened to me and what I was exposed to: abuse, the drag scene, same-sex relationships, the clubs. Those experiences felt like the truest thing about me.

In the middle of all that, the Father met me in a way I didn't expect.

The Question I never thought to Ask

In a prayer ministry session in 2012 — this time I was the one receiving ministry — the prayer minister said something that stopped me in my tracks:

"Why don't you ask God if you're gay?"

I almost laughed.

Duh. Of course I'm gay, I thought. *I'm attracted to men. I've been in same-sex relationships. This has been my life for so long. I'm gay. I'm a drag queen. I'm gay.*

The minister gently repeated, "Why don't you just ask the Holy Spirit?"

So I did.

Inside I was thinking, *Okay, God. You've been with me the whole time. You know. I know.*

It is what it is.

So I said, almost casually, "Okay, God. Am I gay?"

The Voice from My Core

In that moment, a voice came.

Not from outside of me, booming from the heavens, but from my innermost being — from the depths of my core.

And this quiet voice said, "No."

I sat there in shock.

The prayer minister was in shock.

If not, then what?
If not, then who am I?

*I want to say again: this was **my** experience. I am not saying this is what God will say to any other gay person, or that this is how every story should go. I'm simply telling you what happened to me.*

I walked out of that session saying, "Well, I'm never going to get married, God. I'll just be celibate. I don't want to get married."

It was too big to process all at once. The Father had cracked the foundation of what I believed about myself, but the rebuilding would take time.

Six Months Later

Six months later, during morning soaking, the Father very gently said:

"Hey, Lawrence, son. Do you remember when you said, 'I will never get married?'"

"Yeah," I replied.

"Do you think that might be an inner vow?"

"Yes. It is."

So I said, "Okay. I choose to renounce and repent (change my mind) of that vow. I relinquish it. But it's going to take a freaking miracle for me to get married. It's just not my plan."

And the Holy Spirit said:

"Well, I know this guy, Jesus. And He's pretty good with miracles."

I laughed. It was cheeky, kind, disarming.

"What If?"

I said to God, "I don't get it. But whatever You want, I come into agreement with your will."

And the Father said, "Lawrence, what if My plan for you was to get married and have a family?
What if that was the original design and intent for your life?
What if?"

And I remember thinking, *"What if?"*

Not as a theological argument. As an invitation.

For me, that 'what if?' began a slow, gentle re-imagining of my future with God — not forced, not coerced, not driven by shame, but held in love.

The Fruit

Years later, I now have the privilege of ministering to people who need breakthrough and inner healing.

I do not talk them out of their sexuality. I do not try to 'fix' them. I do not offer any kind of conversion or suppression ministry. That is not my lane, and it is not the Father's heart.

What I do is invite them into the same posture I was invited into, an awakening encounter with the Trinity.

Time and time again, I've watched as the Father speaks truth over lies, restores, and reveals original design and intent, in ways that are deeply personal and often very different from my story.

That's the power of the prophetic.

Not just hearing God's voice for information, but hearing His voice for transformation, for restoration, breakthrough, and freedom.

If you're carrying a deep belief about who you are, something you've never dared to question, I want to invite you to do what I did, in your own way and at your own pace:

"Father, is this who I am?
Is this my journey?
Is this Your original design and intent for my life?"

And then listen.

Listen to the voice from your innermost being.
Listen for the tone of Jesus — kind, compassionate, never shaming.

Because that's where the Father speaks.

And when He speaks, everything changes.

Not because someone has forced you into their theology, but because Love Himself has met you in the deepest place of who you are.

[1] *Pastoral note:* Nothing in this story should be read as an endorsement of "conversion therapy," suppression practices, or any attempt to force change on someone's sexuality. I do not offer or recommend that kind of ministry. I am simply describing how God met me personally. Every person's journey with identity, faith, and sexuality is unique and must be approached with humility, consent, safety, and deep compassion.

Learning the Hard Way – When Prophecy Hurts

One thing I've learned the hard way: discernment is rarely meant to be done alone. What we sense God saying is often clarified over time in prayer, in Scripture, and in the presence of wise companions. If you're unsure, bring it to a trusted pastor, spiritual director, supervisor, or mature friend. Let love, peace, and fruit be part of the test.

In 2011, as I was learning to hear from God, I got very excited.

I realised I could hear Him. I could bless people by sharing His heart. Those first couple of years, I wanted to prophesy over everyone — people in cafés, at bus stops, anywhere.

But here's what I've learned:

We must know God's heart for ourselves, before we try to share His heart with others.

Not just operating in the gift, but knowing the Gift Giver.

The Moment I Got It Wrong

I started getting 'downloads' about people, vulnerable, intimate things.

In my naivety, I assumed God was showing me these things I could share with them. If I knew it, surely He wanted me to say it, right?

Then one day, I shared something I'd sensed about someone, something deeply personal.

It wasn't received well.

In fact, it hurt them.

I walked away thinking, *How did I get this wrong? I was so sure I heard from God.*

The Father's Correction

I sat with the Trinity and asked, "How did I get this wrong?"

The Father came, put His arm around me, and said:

"Lawrence, son, I share things with you not always to share vocally, but to pray.
To intercede.
To understand what is going on for that person.
To learn empathy.
Empathy is entering into what that person is experiencing, not just feeling sorry for them, but understanding My heart for them."

In that moment, the Holy Spirit brought a deep conviction and said:

"Lawrence, only do what I ask you to do.
Only say what I ask you to say.
That's it — from now on."

The Freedom That Came

That word freed me.

I didn't have to come up with a prophetic word for every person I met. The pressure came off.

Unless He said, "Speak," I could simply rest. Be present. Pray quietly.

I realised there was something in me, an unmet need for affirmation, for approval, for the thrill of 'getting it right.'

I was using the prophetic to meet my own needs.

Yes, I was good at it. Yes, it felt good.

But it was still coming from the wrong place.

Now, when I share the Father's heart with people, it's a joy.

Not because I need to prove myself or demonstrate my prophetic gifting.

But because He's asking.

I'm grounded in my identity as a son, a king, a priest, an ambassador of the kingdom — shifting atmospheres wherever I go, walking in my Father's authority, bringing heaven to earth.

The prophetic isn't about me.

It's about Him.

And when I operate from that place, from rest, identity, and sonship, the prophetic flows with purity, power, and purpose.

The Lesson

If you're stepping into the prophetic and you get it wrong — and you will — don't be discouraged.

Don't let shame silence you.

Let the Father correct you. Let the Holy Spirit refine you.

Ask Him:

"Why did You show me this?
Was it to share, or was it to pray?"

Then only do what He asks you to do.

Only say what He asks you to say.

That's the key to operating in the prophetic with purity and power.

Not from unmet needs. Not from the approval of people. Not from the excitement of being right.

But from rest. From identity. From sonship.

The Prophetic Is for Everyone

Here's what I want you to hear: the prophetic isn't just for 'prophets.'

It's for everyone who is filled with the Father's love.
Everyone who is soaking in His presence.
Everyone who is resting in His heart.

You can hear God's voice.
You can share His heart.
You can speak life over others.

Not because you're special.

But because you're His.

And when you're full of Him, you naturally leak Him over others.

That's prophetic leaking.

Prophecy Flows from Love

Paul says in 1 Corinthians 14:1

"Pursue love, and earnestly desire the spiritual gifts, especially that you may prophesy."

Notice the order: pursue love first. Then desire the gifts.

Because prophecy that doesn't flow from love is just noise.

Prophecy that flows from love brings life, healing, restoration, and hope.

That's the prophetic we're after.

Not impressive words. Not spiritual performance.

Love made manifest through words.

Learning to Hear His Voice (Practical Steps)

How do you hear God's voice? Here are some simple steps:

1. **Spend time in His presence.**

   You can't leak what you're not soaking in. Rest with Him. Let Him fill you.

2. **Ask Him to speak.**

   God loves to speak. Ask — and then listen.

3. **Pay attention to what you sense.**

   He may speak through words, pictures, impressions, Scripture, or a deep knowing. Notice what stirs.

4. **Test it.**

   Does it align with Scripture? Does it sound like the Father's heart? Does it bring life, not shame?

5. **Step out in faith.**

   Start small. Share gently. Use language like, "I wonder if God might be saying…" Trust the Holy Spirit to guide you.

6. **Learn from mistakes.**

   When you miss it, let Him correct you. Stay humble. Keep going. Failure is part of formation, not disqualification.

The prophetic is not about having a platform.

It's an invitation for people to encounter the Father's love, see themselves as He sees them, and step into their identity, calling, and destiny.

HEART WORK

Reflection, Prayer, and Encounter

Scripture

"I am the sprouting vine and you're my branches. As you live in union with me as your source, fruitfulness will stream from within you."

— John 15:5a (TPT)

"I am the Vine, you are the branches. When you're joined with me and I with you, the relation intimate and organic, the harvest is sure to be abundant."

— John 15:5 (The Message)

Reflection Questions

Choose 1-3 questions that stand out to you today. You don't need to answer them all.

If you're reading in a group, you may choose one question to share and keep the rest private.

- Have you ever experienced 'prophetic leaking' — where God's heart for someone just overflowed out of you? What happened?

- What deep beliefs about your identity might you need to ask God about, like I did with 'Am I?'

- Have you ever gotten a prophetic word wrong or shared something prematurely? How did you respond?

- Are you operating in the prophetic from rest and sonship, or from a need for approval and significance?

- What would it look like for you to only say what God asks you to say, and to keep the rest for prayer?

Journal Prompt

"When I sense God's heart for someone, I feel… and I'm afraid that…"

Write honestly about your experience with the prophetic — the joy, the fear, the mistakes, the pressure. Then ask Jesus, "What does it look like to prophesy from overflow, not striving?"

Your Reflections:

One Thing to Try This Week

Ask the Father to show you His heart for one person in your life. Write down what you sense — but don't share it yet. Pray it over them first. Then ask, "Do You want me to share this, or just intercede?"

Breath Prayer for This Week

Inhale: "I remain in You"
Exhale: "You overflow through me"

Let this truth root your prophetic gifting in union, not performance.

Soaking Exercise
Prophesying from the Overflow

1. Find a quiet space and invite the Holy Spirit to lead you.
2. Close your eyes and take a few deep breaths. Let yourself rest in His presence.
3. Picture yourself as a branch connected to the vine (Jesus). You're not striving or producing — just abiding.
4. Ask Him, "What is flowing through me when I'm connected to You?"
5. Now think of one person in your life. Ask Jesus, "What is Your heart for them?"
6. Wait. Don't force it. Notice any words, images, feelings, or Scriptures that come.
7. If nothing comes, that's okay. Just rest in the connection.
8. If something does come, ask Him, "Is this for me to share, or for me to pray?"

9. Thank Him for letting you carry His heart, even if you never speak a word.

What did you notice?

Prayer

Jesus,
Thank You for letting me carry Your heart for others.
Thank You that the prophetic is not about being impressive,
it's about being connected to You.

Forgive me for the times I've spoken from insecurity,
from a need to be seen or significant,
or from pressure to perform.

May I learn to prophesy from union and overflow, not striving.
May I learn to remain in You, so that fruitfulness streams naturally.
May I learn when to speak and when to keep praying.

Heal any wounds I've carried from getting it wrong,
or from being misunderstood.

Root my gifting in Your love, not in people's approval.

I am Your branch.
You are my source.
Let Your heart leak through me.

Let it be so.

Amen.

PART III

HEART KEYS: HEALING FROM THE INSIDE OUT

PREFACE

Up to this point, you've been walking with me through the long ache of father wounds, the places of shame and searching, and the slow, surprising way the Father met me with love I couldn't earn and couldn't outrun.

Parts I and II are deeply personal because that's where healing begins, in the real places, with real names, real memories, and real encounters with God.

But healing doesn't end with an encounter.

Love received becomes love embodied.

What the Father restores in us, He often begins to release through us, not as a performance, not as a platform, but as a quiet overflow of grace.

Part III is where the story turns outward.

Some readers will want to stay in the narrative and keep moving. I get that — I'm wired that way too. So let me say this clearly: what follows isn't a detour from the story.

'It's the why underneath it.' These pages are here because they became part of my own healing; they're the way I learned to walk with others gently, safely, and well.

Here I introduce **Heart Keys**, the inner healing ministry that grew out of my own journey and the journeys of many others I've had the privilege to walk alongside.

This is not a formula and it's not a replacement for professional counselling. It's a Spirit-led, trauma-aware, consent-based way of making room for Jesus to come close to the places we've learned to hide, so that truth can be heard, wounds can be tended, and hearts can begin to breathe again.

You'll find two movements in this section. First, I'll share the foundations: what **Heart Keys** is, what it isn't, and the values that shape how we minister. Then I'll offer stories from the healing room. They're here not to impress you, but to give you hope: that God still restores, that people really can change, and that even long-held pain can become a place of encounter.

If you're reading this as someone who is wounded, my invitation is simple: go gently. Take your time. You are not behind. There is no rush in the kingdom.

If you find yourself needing to pause, skip ahead, or come back later, that's okay — this is not meant to be rushed.

And if you're reading as a leader, pastor, caregiver, or friend who wants to help others well, my invitation is also simple: let love lead.

The goal is never to 'fix' someone. The goal is to create a safe space where the Healer can come.

Welcome to the healing room.

CHAPTER 9

HEART KEYS – HEALING FROM THE INSIDE OUT

One Healed Heart

Before I tell you more stories from the healing room, I want to give you the foundations — because safety matters, and love needs a language.

If **Heart Keys** has a 'method,' it's simply this: we make room for the Trinity to come close to the places we've learned to hide.

Then we watch what happens when love is allowed to lead.

One healed heart can change a family.
One healed heart can change a community.
One healed heart can change a generation.

That's the power of inner healing.

And that's the vision behind **Heart Keys**.

The Vision

After my awakening encounter with the Father at the **School of Ministry**, and years of receiving prayer ministry and experiencing deep healing, I knew I was called to help others experience the same.

Not just to receive healing for myself, but to become a conduit of healing for others.

That's how **Heart Keys** was born.

Heart Keys is a ministry dedicated to inner healing and heart transformation. We partner with the Trinity to bring healing to the deep wounds of the heart — the wounds that shape how we see ourselves, how we see God, and how we see the world.

Because one healed heart changes everything.

The Biblical Foundation

This isn't theory for me — it's the heartbeat of Jesus, and it's what I've seen Him do again and again.

The foundation of **Heart Keys** is built on these truths:

"I will give him the key to the house of David-the highest position in the royal court. When he opens doors, no one will be able to close them; when he closes doors, no one will be able to open them." Isaiah 22:22 (NLT)

"The Sovereign LORD has filled me with his Spirit. He has chosen me and sent me To bring good news to the poor, To heal the brokenhearted, To announce release to captives And freedom to those in prison." Isaiah 61:1 (GNT)

These are not just nice verses for fridge magnets.

This is the mission of Jesus.

And it's the mission He's invited us into.

Jesus didn't just heal bodies or cast out demons. He healed hearts.

- The woman at the well (John 4) – He addressed her shame and identity.

- The woman caught in adultery (John 8) – He addressed her condemnation.
- Peter after the denial (John 21) – He restored his heart and calling.

Jesus is a heart healer.

What Is Prayer Ministry or Heart Healing?

Prayer ministry — also called inner healing or heart healing, — is a process of inviting the Holy Spirit to reveal and heal the deep parts and wounds of the heart.[2]

- It's not counselling (though it can be therapeutic).
- It's not deliverance in a dramatic sense (though deliverance can happen).
- It's not spiritual direction (though it can be deeply formational).

At its core, it's partnering with the Trinity to bring healing to the places in your heart that are broken, wounded, and in need of the Father's love.

Partnering with the Trinity

Heart healing is not about me fixing you or having all the answers.

It's about partnering with the Trinity.

- The Father reveals the wound.
- Jesus brings the healing.
- The Holy Spirit applies the truth.

---

[2] A gentle reminder: this book (and Heart Keys prayer ministry) isn't a substitute for professional mental health care. If you're dealing with trauma symptoms, flashbacks, or feeling unsafe, it can be wise to seek qualified support alongside your spiritual journey.

My role is simply to facilitate. To ask gentle questions. To create a safe space. To invite the Trinity into the process.

The Trinity does the work. I just get to be present.

The Journey of the Heart

The heart is the centre of who we are.

Proverbs 4:23 says:

"Above all else, guard your heart,
for everything you do flows from it."

Not your mind. Not your behaviour.

Your heart.

What's in your heart shapes everything.

- If your heart is wounded, your life will reflect that.
- If your heart is healed, your life will reflect that too.

That's why the heart matters. That's why inner healing matters.

Heart healing isn't 'new age.' It's deeply biblical and deeply human, allowing God to meet us in the places that have shaped our story.

Healing vs Miracles

There's a difference between healing and miracles.

A **miracle** is instant. One moment you're sick, the next you're healed. One moment you're bound, the next you're free.

Healing is a process. It takes time. It requires partnership. It involves layers.

Both are valid. Both are biblical. Both are needed.

But when it comes to the heart, healing is usually a process. The wounds didn't happen overnight. The healing usually doesn't either.

Still, the Father is patient and committed.

Layer by layer. Memory by memory. Lie by lie.

He is in it for the long haul.

God Doesn't Just Heal Memories. He Enters Them.

One of the most powerful aspects of inner healing is this:

God doesn't just heal the memory.

He goes back into the memory and heals that moment in time.

He doesn't just comfort you in the present about what happened in the past.

He meets you in the past.

Not by changing the facts, but by changing your experience of them.

How This Works

In prayer ministry, we invite the Holy Spirit to flow wherever the experience or memory needs to go, and allow the Trinity to love and bring life to what needs healing.

Then we ask, "Jesus, where were You in this moment?"

Time and time again, Jesus shows up in this experience, not as a distant observer, but as a participant. He was there. He's always been there.

When you see Him in the memory, when you experience His presence in that moment — the wound begins to heal, because the lie that was planted there is replaced with the truth of His presence.

My Own Experience

I remember a prayer ministry session where the Holy Spirit brought up a memory of being molested as a child.

It was a memory I'd buried for years. A memory I didn't want to revisit.

But the Holy Spirit gently brought it up, and the prayer minister asked, "Lawrence, where was Jesus in that moment?"

I looked. And I saw Him.

He was there.

Not standing at a distance. Not looking away in disgust.

He was holding me.

He was weeping with me. He was angry at what was being done to me. He was protecting my heart even when my body couldn't be protected.

In that moment, the lie that "I was alone, that it was my fault, that I was dirty," was shattered.

Because I wasn't alone.

And that changed everything.

Inner healing is a journey, not a one-time event. There are layers. There are multiple memories. There are different wounds. But each time you invite Jesus into the journey, each time you see where He was, each time you hear His truth over the lie — healing happens.

Forgiveness: A Key to Healing

One of the most important aspects of inner healing is forgiveness.

Not because the person who hurt you deserves it.

Because you deserve to be free.

Unforgiveness is like drinking poison and expecting the other person to die. It keeps you bound. It keeps you stuck. It keeps the wound open.

Forgiveness is the key that unlocks the prison.

What Forgiveness Is (and Isn't)

Forgiveness is **not**:

- Saying what they did was okay.
- Excusing their behaviour.
- Pretending it didn't hurt.
- Reconciling with someone who is unsafe.
- Forgetting what happened.

Forgiveness **is**:

- Releasing them from the debt they owe you.
- Choosing not to hold it against them anymore.
- Handing them over to God.
- Setting yourself free from bitterness.
- Trusting God to be the King and Father (not judge).

Forgiveness is for you, not for them. It doesn't erase justice; it hands justice back to God. Not man's version of justice, but our Father's version.

When Wounds Braid Together: The Three-Stranded Cord

Another significant aspect of my own healing journey has been facing how deeply my dad's departure affected me.

Rejection.
Abandonment.
Loss.

These weren't just passing emotions; they were wounds that had taken up residence in my heart. And when wounds stay longer than they should, when they're not attended to, they start to manifest in other ways.

Over time, I began to notice a pattern:

- Rejection often showed up as **anger**.
- Abandonment partnered with **fear**.
- Loss expressed itself through **grief**.

So I wasn't just dealing with rejection, abandonment, and loss. I was also wrestling with anger, fear, and grief. It felt like a rope I could never break.

I'd get some breakthrough around rejection, and then anger would flare again. I'd work through abandonment, and suddenly loss would surface. No matter how much I twisted and turned, the rope just seemed to tighten.

The Holy Spirit began to use a picture from Scripture to help me understand what was happening.

Ecclesiastes 4:12 says:

"Though one may be overpowered,
two can defend themselves.
A cord of three strands is not quickly broken."

We often use this verse to talk about the strength of unity — a three-stranded cord being stronger than a single strand. In a spiritual context, it reminds us of the power of journeying with God, knowing ourselves, and walking with our brothers and sisters.

But I began to see that the enemy also loves to braid things together.

Just as God can weave a three-stranded cord for our good, there can also be a dark, counterfeit cord at work in our lives.

In my story, it looked like this:

- **Rejection, abandonment, and loss** braided together with
- **Anger, fear, and grief**

That's six separate realities, but they were operating like a single rope around my heart. No wonder it felt so hard to get free.

This revelation was profound for me — both in my own deliverance and in walking with others in the heart healing space.

Suddenly, things made sense:

- "I've dealt with the rejection. I've forgiven. Why am I still so angry?"
- "I've processed the abandonment. Why is this fear still here?"
- "I've grieved the loss. Why does the grief keep coming back?"

Often, it wasn't that they had done something wrong. It was that they were dealing with one strand of a cord, while the other strands were still tightly woven around it.

When we began to name and address all of it — rejection, abandonment, loss, and the anger, fear, and grief attached to them — things started to shift. There was new clarity, less frustration, and a deeper level of freedom.

The good news is this:

The same way a three-stranded cord can work against us, a three-stranded cord can also work for us.

When we:

- journey honestly with God;
- grow in knowing ourselves; and
- allow trusted brothers and sisters to walk with us;

a different kind of braid forms — a cord of healing, transformation, and restoration.

The rope that once bound us becomes a testimony of what love can untangle.

Restoration to Original Design

The goal of inner healing isn't just to heal the wound.

The goal is to restore you to your **original design**.

To who you were created to be before the wounds, before the lies, before the trauma.

God is not just trying to make you functional.

He's restoring you to wholeness.

Not just managing the pain, but restoring the glory.

Restoring Identity Through Healing

So much of inner healing is about identity restoration.

Because the wounds we carry shape how we see ourselves.

- The abuse says, "You're dirty."

- The abandonment says, "You're not wanted."
- The rejection says, "You're not enough."

We believe those lies. We build our identity around them.

But that's not who you are.

Inner healing is the process of dismantling the false identity and restoring the true one — the identity that the Father has always been whispering deep into your spirit:

"You are Mine. You are loved. You are wanted. You are enough. You are beautiful. You are worthy. You are My masterpiece."

That's who you are.

And inner healing helps your heart finally believe it.

The Power of Encounter and the Ministry of Presence

At the end of the day, inner healing is about an awakening **encounter**.

Not just information. Not just theology. Not just technique.

Encounter with the Father.
Encounter with Jesus.
Encounter with the Holy Spirit.

It's in the encounter that everything changes.

- It's in the encounter that lies are shattered.
- It's in the encounter that wounds are healed.
- It's in the encounter that identity is restored.

In prayer ministry, my role is simple: to be present.

Not to fix. Not to have all the answers. Not to perform.

Just to be present.

To create space for the Holy Spirit to work.
To ask questions that invite revelation.
To hold space for grief, for anger, for confusion.
To bear witness to the Father's love.

That's the ministry of presence.

And it's one of the most powerful things we can offer.

Why the Heart Matters (Again)

The heart is the centre of who we are.

Proverbs 4:23 says:

"Above all else, guard your heart,
for everything you do flows from it."

What's in your heart shapes everything.

- If your heart believes you're unloved, you'll live like you're unloved.
- If your heart believes you're unworthy, you'll live like you're unworthy.
- If your heart believes you're broken, you'll live like you're broken.

But if your heart believes you're loved, wanted, valued, and cherished, everything changes.

That's why the heart matters.
That's why inner healing matters.

Because healed hearts change everything.

Healed Hearts Change Everything

One healed heart can change a family.
When you're healed, you stop passing down the wounds to the next generation.

One healed heart can change a community.
When you're healed, you can love others from wholeness, not brokenness.

One healed heart can change a generation.
When you're healed, you break the cycles and create new patterns.

That's the power of one healed heart.

The Ripple Effect

Healing isn't just for you. It's for everyone around you.

- When you're healed, your relationships shift.
- When you're healed, your ministry becomes healthier.
- When you're healed, your family is impacted.
- When you're healed, your community is transformed.

That's the ripple effect.

One healed heart creates waves that reach far beyond what you can see.

The Invitation

For some of us, the idea of Jesus being present in a traumatic memory can feel impossible or even upsetting. This isn't about pretending the harm was okay, or suggesting God wanted it. It's an invitation to awaken and gently ask, "Jesus, where were You, and what were You doing toward me?" If that question feels too much right now, honour that. Healing is not forced, and God is not offended by your honesty.

I want to invite you to let the Father heal your heart.

Not just manage the pain. Not just cope with the wounds.

Heal.

Invite the Holy Spirit to reveal the root wound.
Invite Jesus into the memories that need healing.
Invite the Father to speak truth over the lies you've believed.

You don't have to carry it anymore.

The Father has always been waiting with open arms, healing in His hands, and love in His eyes.

Come and be healed.

HEART WORK

Reflection, Prayer, and Encounter

Scripture

"He heals the wounds of every shattered heart."

— Psalm 147:3 (TPT)

"He heals the broken-hearted and bandages their wounds."

— Psalm 147:3 (The Remedy)

Reflection Questions

Choose 1-3 questions that stand out to you today. You don't need to answer them all.

If you're reading in a group, you may choose one question to share and keep the rest private.

- What wounds are you carrying that need the Father's healing touch?

- Have you ever invited Jesus into a painful memory? What happened — or what do you fear might happen?

- Who do you need to forgive? What is holding you back from releasing them?

- Where do you see 'braided' patterns like rejection/abandonment/loss and anger/fear/grief in your own story?

- What lies have you believed about yourself because of past wounds?

- What would it look like for you to be restored to your original design?

Journal Prompt

"The wound I've carried the longest is… and the lie it planted in me is…"

Write honestly about the pain. Then ask Jesus, "Where were You in that moment? What is the truth You want to speak over this wound?"

Your Reflections:

One Thing to Try This Week

Identify one person you need to forgive — not because they deserve it, but because you want to be free. Write their name down and say out loud, "I choose to release [name] into Your hands, Father. I don't want to carry this anymore."

Breath Prayer for This Week

Inhale: "You heal my heart"
Exhale: "From the inside out"

Let this truth reach the places you've protected or hidden.

Soaking Exercise[3]
Inviting Jesus Into a Memory

1. Find a safe, quiet space. Invite the Holy Spirit to guide you gently and only as far as is safe.

2. Close your eyes and take a few deep breaths. Ask for His protection and presence.

3. Ask Jesus, "Is there a memory You want to heal today?" Wait. Let Him bring something to the surface — don't force it.

4. If a memory comes, picture it like a scene. Notice where you are, how old you are, what's happening.

---

[3] This practice is an invitation, not a demand. It's not a claim that God caused the harm, wanted it, or called it "good." It's simply a gentle question: "Jesus, where were You, and what were You doing toward me?" If that feels too much right now, please honour your pace, and consider doing this with a trusted companion or qualified support.

5. Don't rush past the pain. Let yourself feel it. Then ask, "Jesus, where were You in this moment?"

6. Wait. Let Him show you. He may be holding you, standing between you and harm, weeping with you, or speaking truth.

7. Ask Him, "What do You want me to know? What is the truth about me in this moment?"

8. If a lie surfaces (e.g., "I'm worthless," "It's my fault," or "I'm alone"), ask Him to replace it with His truth.

9. Rest in His presence. Thank Him for being there — then and now.

What did you notice?

Prayer

Jesus,
You know every wound I carry,
the ones I talk about and the ones I've buried deep.

I invite You into the broken parts today.
Show me where You were when I was hurt.
Speak truth over the lies I've believed about myself.

Heal my heart from the inside out —
not with a quick fix, but with Your patient, layered love.

Give me the courage to forgive those who wounded me,
not because they deserve it,
but because I want to be free.

Restore me to my original design.
Remind me of who I was before the world told me who to be.

I trust You with my story.
Heal me, Jesus.

Let it be so.

Amen.

CHAPTER 10

STORIES FROM THE HEALING ROOM

When I say 'the healing room,' I don't mean a place with special power. I mean any space, a lounge room, an office, a church hall, where we make room for Jesus to meet a person with tenderness, love, and truth.

Inner healing can sound abstract until you see it in real lives.

The stories in this chapter are true, but I've changed names and identifying details to protect privacy. They're not formulas or guarantees, just glimpses of what can happen when people bring their hearts to the Father and allow Him to meet them there.

Emma – "Why Did Dad Leave?"

Emma was a young woman in ministry, gifted and passionate. From the outside, she was thriving, leading worship, serving faithfully, always available for others.

Inside, she was terrified of being left.

Her dad had walked out when she was young. No explanation, no closure. One day he was there; the next day he wasn't. Her body grew up, but part of her heart stayed eight years old, still waiting for him to come back.

In our first prayer ministry session, she said, "I know God loves me, but I always feel like He's about to change His mind."

We invited the Holy Spirit to highlight an experience that connected to that feeling. A scene came up: her dad's car driving away, her mum sobbing in the kitchen, Emma standing in the driveway, frozen.

We asked, "Jesus, where were You in that moment?"

At first, she saw nothing, just the car, the dust, the ache in her chest. Then slowly, she began to weep.

"I can see Him," she whispered. "He's kneeling next to me in the driveway. He's got His arm around me. He's crying with me."

We stayed there for a while. No rush. No pressure. Just presence.

Then we asked, "Jesus, what do You want Emma to know about this moment?"

Through tears, she said, "He's saying, 'I didn't leave. I never left. Your dad walked away, but I stayed. You were never alone.'"

The lie that had lodged itself in that memory 'I'm not worth staying for' — began to crumble.

Later, we gently led her through forgiveness. Not excusing her father, not pretending it didn't hurt, but releasing him from the debt he could never repay and handing him over to God.

Over the months that followed, the fruit showed up in quiet ways:

- She stopped apologising for existing in every conversation.

- She began to risk deeper friendships without panicking at the first sign of distance.
- Worship became less about trying to convince God to come close and more about resting in the God who had never left.

One healed heart began to change the way she led, loved, and lived.

Daniel – Pornography, Anxiety, and the Need to Numb

Daniel was a young male pastor in his twenties — smart, funny, serving in his church, loved by his community.

He was also addicted to pornography.

He'd tried everything: filters, accountability, fasting, self-hatred. Nothing worked for long. The shame was crushing. Every time he slipped, he promised God he'd 'try harder,' then fell again.

When we met, I didn't start with the behaviour. I started with his heart.

"When do you most feel the pull toward porn?" I asked.

"Late at night," he said. "When I'm exhausted. When I feel like I've failed. When I'm alone."

We invited Holy Spirit into that pattern.

"Jesus, what's really going on in those moments?"

As we waited, he said quietly, "I feel like a little boy who's been yelled at all day. Porn is the only place I feel like no one is judging me. It's twisted, but it feels like comfort."

There it was: not just lust, but a desperate need for comfort and kindness.

We asked Jesus to show him where that need began. An experience surfaced of being a child, bringing home a report card that wasn't perfect, and being mocked and shamed. The message he absorbed was: You're only safe when you perform. When you fail, you deserve punishment.

In that experience, we asked, "Jesus, where are You?"

He saw Jesus sitting next to him on the bed, taking the report card, smiling.

"He's saying, 'I'm proud of you. You're not a grade. You're My boy.'"

We didn't pray, "God, take away his sexuality." We prayed, "Father, meet the need that porn has been trying to meet. Be his comfort. Be his safe place."

Over time, Daniel began to:

- Notice the early signs of anxiety and bring them to God before they escalated.
- Reach out to safe friends instead of isolating.
- Practise soaking, letting the Father say, "I love you," instead of punishing himself.

The temptation didn't vanish overnight, but the power of it weakened as the root need — comfort and acceptance — was met in a healthier way.

Freedom came not just through willpower, but through encounter.

A Pastor in the Middle – "I Can't Tell Anyone This"

Another story comes from a local pastor I'll call 'Mark.'

Mark loved his church. He preached grace, led faithfully, and genuinely cared for his people. But he carried a secret: he was burnt out, angry, and fantasising about walking away from ministry altogether.

"I can't tell my board," he said. "They'd panic. I can't tell my congregation; they'd lose trust. I can't tell my family; they're already carrying so much. I feel trapped."

This is where **Heart Keys** and pastoral supervision overlap.

In our sessions, we didn't just talk about his sermon schedule or leadership challenges. We talked about his heart.

We explored:

- The grief he'd never processed from a previous church split.
- The resentment he felt when people treated him like a spiritual vending machine.
- The fear that if he ever stopped performing, he'd be replaced.

We invited Jesus into this space where he'd been publicly criticised by a senior leader years earlier. In that moment, he'd made an inner vow: I will never show weakness again.

As he saw Jesus standing beside him in that experience — eyes full of compassion, not contempt — he was able to renounce that vow and allow himself to be human again.

Practically, he made changes:

- He took a proper Sabbath for the first time in years.
- He began seeing a counsellor alongside supervision.
- He let a trusted friend know the truth about his exhaustion.

He didn't quit ministry. He did, however, begin to lead from a different place, not as an untouchable hero, but as a beloved son with limits.

His church didn't collapse when he became more honest. If anything, it became healthier, because their pastor was no longer ministering from emptiness.

Not a Formula, but a Pattern

Every story is different.

- Some people experience dramatic encounters in a single session.
- Others walk a slow, gentle journey over months or years.
- Some see immediate changes in behaviour; others notice subtle shifts in how they think, feel, and relate.

There is no formula. But there is a pattern:

1. An honest cry – "Something in me needs healing."
2. An invitation – "Holy Spirit, what do You want to show me?"
3. A memory or theme surfaces — often surprising, sometimes familiar.
4. Jesus reveals His presence and truth in that place.
5. Lies are exposed, forgiveness is offered, and identity is restored.
6. New fruit emerges — not from striving, but from a healed root.

That's **Heart Keys** in real life.

Your Story

You might not relate to Emma's father wound, Daniel's pornography battle, or Mark's pastoral burnout.

Your story might involve:

- A friendship betrayal that still shapes how you trust.

- A church experience that left you wary of leaders.
- A childhood of being "the responsible one" who never got to have needs.
- A secret addiction, a hidden grief, or a shame you've never spoken aloud.

Whatever your story, the same invitation stands:

"Jesus, where are You in this?
What do You want me to know?
What lie did I believe here?
What is the truth?"

Inner healing isn't about digging endlessly for pain. It's about following the gentle lead of the Holy Spirit to the places He's already highlighting, and letting Him do what He loves to do:

Heal hearts.
Restore identity.
Bring sons and daughters home.

HEART WORK

Reflection, Prayer, and Encounter

Scripture

"The Spirit of the Lord Yahweh is upon me, because he has anointed me to preach good news to the poor. He has sent me to heal the broken-hearted and to tell captives, 'You are free!' and to prisoners, 'You are forgiven and restored!'"

— Isaiah 61:1 (TPT)

"God's Spirit is on me; he's chosen me to preach the Message of good news to the poor, sent me to announce pardon to prisoners and recovery of sight to the blind, to set the burdened and battered free."

— Luke 4:18 (The Message)

Reflection Questions

Choose 1-3 questions that stand out to you today. You don't need to answer them all.

If you're reading in a group, you may choose one question to share and keep the rest private.

- Which story in this chapter resonated with you most, Emma, Daniel, Mark, or another? Why?

- Where do you see similar patterns in your own life (e.g. fear of abandonment, using comfort to numb pain, burnout)?

- If Jesus stepped into one of your painful memories today, what do you imagine He might do or say?
- Are there inner vows you've made ("I'll never trust again," or, "I have to do it all myself.") that God is inviting you to revisit?
- Who is one safe person you could invite into your healing journey?

Journal Prompt

"The story I most relate to is… because underneath, I've been carrying…"

Write about the feelings beneath your story — the fear, the shame, the loneliness, the striving. Then ask Jesus, "What do You want to heal in me?"

Your Reflections:

One Thing to Try This Week

Identify one inner vow you've made (e.g., "I'll never let anyone hurt me again," or, "I have to be strong for everyone."). Write it down, then say out loud, "I renounce this vow. I invite You, Jesus, to show me a better way."

Breath Prayer for This Week

Inhale: "You see my story"
Exhale: "You heal my heart"

Let this truth quiet the voice that says you're too broken or too far gone.

Soaking Exercise

Your Story in the Healing Room

1. Find a quiet, safe space. Invite the Holy Spirit to lead you gently.

2. Close your eyes and take a few deep breaths. Let yourself settle.

3. Picture yourself in a healing room. It's safe, warm, and peaceful. Jesus is there with you.

4. Ask Him, "What story do You want to heal in me today?" Wait. Let a memory, feeling, or pattern surface.

5. If something comes, don't judge it or rush past it. Just notice it.

6. Ask Jesus, "What is the lie I've believed because of this?" Let Him show you.

7. Now ask, "What is the truth You want to speak over me?"

8. If an inner vow surfaces (e.g., "I'll never trust again."), ask Him, "What would You have me do instead?"

9. Rest in His presence. Let Him heal, restore, and speak identity over you.

What did you notice?

Prayer

Jesus,
Thank You for the stories in this chapter,
for Emma, Daniel, Mark, and all the others
who have let You into their pain.

I see myself in their stories.
I see the patterns, the wounds, the vows, the shame.

I invite You into my story today.
Show me the lies I've believed.
Speak truth over the broken places.
Help me renounce the vows that have kept me stuck.

Give me courage to be honest,
with You, with myself, and with at least one safe person.

Heal my heart, Jesus.
Restore my identity.
Set me free.

I trust You with my story.

Let it be so.

Amen.

As I watched God heal hearts, I began to notice something else: the people who carry others often carry pain quietly. Many leaders are faithful and gifted, yet exhausted and alone. In the next section, I want to turn toward them, because caring for caregivers isn't a side topic. It's part of how healing becomes a culture.

PART IV

CARING FOR THE CAREGIVERS

PREFACE

You may notice some themes returning here. That's intentional. The same wounds show up in different clothing as we grow — first in our personal story, then in how we lead, relate, and build culture. This is the same river, just a different bank.

If Part III is about how God restores hearts, Part IV is about something just as important: how we care for the people who carry others.

Many leaders, pastors, ministry workers, chaplains, spiritual directors, and caregivers are quietly exhausted. They're faithful, prayerful, and still showing up, but inside they may be running on fumes. Some have learned to cope with pain rather than process it. Some have never had a truly safe place to be honest. And some have been wounded in the very spaces that were meant to nurture them.

I've seen this up close in others, and in myself. The Church needs leaders who are not just gifted, but whole. Not perfect, but honest. Not invulnerable, but well-supported. Because the cost of unprocessed pain in leadership is high: it leaks into relationships, decision-making, team culture, and even theology. And yet the solution isn't shame or pressure. The solution is the same way God heals all of us: presence, truth, tenderness, and time.

Part IV is written for those who lead and those who love leaders. It's about cultivating safe spaces, places where Jesus is not an idea, but a real presence in the room; where people can exhale; where the masks can come off; where discernment is possible again; where leaders are cared for as human beings, not just as functions.

You'll read about the kind of environment that makes healing possible for caregivers: confidentiality, non-judgement, consent, wise boundaries, and Spirit-led compassion. You'll also find practical wisdom from the **Heart Keys** approach applied specifically to leaders, because the needs of caregivers are often unique, and the stakes are often higher.

If you're a leader reading this, I want you to hear this clearly: you are allowed to need care. You are allowed to have limits. You are allowed to be in process. And you are worthy of the same gentleness you offer others.

And if you're someone who supports leaders, my hope is that these chapters will help you create spaces where the strong can be honest, the tired can rest, and the hidden places can be met with grace.

Because when leaders are cared for, communities become safer. And when communities become safer, healing multiplies.

Welcome to the work of caring for the caregivers.

CHAPTER 11

SAFE SPACES FOR LEADERS - JESUS IN THE ROOM

Leaders are often the last people allowed to be human.

They're the ones people run to when life falls apart, the ones who hold the stories, pray the prayers, preach the sermons, and keep the wheels turning. And from the outside, they often look strong.

But behind the microphone, many are quietly running on empty.

This chapter is for them. And it's also for those who love them.

It's about the pastors, worship leaders, missionaries, chaplains, small-group leaders, and ministry pioneers who have learned to hold everyone else's pain while hiding their own. It's about the hidden world of leaders and the safe spaces they desperately need.

The Leader Who Couldn't Breathe

I still remember the way his shoulders shook.

He was a well-known pastor, the kind whose name appeared on conference flyers and whose sermons were shared around the world. But in my small office, with the door closed and the blinds half-drawn, he looked less like a spiritual giant and more like a man who had forgotten how to breathe.

"I can't do this anymore, Lawrence," he whispered. "I don't know who to tell. I don't even know if I'm allowed to be this tired."

There were no cameras, no elders' meetings, no stage lights — just a man, his breaking heart, and Jesus in the room.

We sat in silence for a while. His hands trembled. Years of uncried tears began to surface. He wasn't confessing a scandal; he was confessing his humanity.

"I preach grace every week," he said, "but I don't know where to go when I need it."

That sentence has stayed with me.

The Hidden World of Leaders

Most people see the microphone, not the migraines. They see the full auditorium, not the empty kitchen table when the pastor gets home. They see the polished sermon, not the Saturday night anxiety. They see the confident worship leader, not the panic attack in the car park.

Leaders are trained to hold other people's stories, but very few are ever taught what to do with their own. They become experts at creating rooms where everyone else can cry, confess, or collapse, but they don't know where to go when it's their turn.

I've sat with leaders who:

- haven't had a real day off in months (sometimes years).
- are carrying grief from church splits, betrayals, or failures in their teams.
- are terrified that if they admit they're struggling, they'll lose their job, their income, or the trust of their people.
- have become so used to being the strong one that they don't know how to be anything else.

By the time a headline uses the words 'moral failure,' something else has often been failing for a long time.

Long before a leader crosses a line with money, sex, or power, they have often crossed a quieter line — the moment they stopped being honest about their pain. They stopped telling the truth about their exhaustion, their loneliness, their temptations. They stopped having a room where they could be fully human.

The Church is often shocked by the scandal. It would appear that Heaven would be more grieved by the years of unattended pain.

When Care Fails Before Morals Do

None of this removes responsibility. Choices matter. Boundaries matter. Accountability matters.

But I have become convinced that what we often call moral failure is, at its root, a care failure.

Somewhere along the way, a leader stopped resting, stopped grieving, stopped telling the truth, and/or stopped being a son or daughter and became a role.

They became a brand, a function, a set of expectations. They learned to survive on adrenaline, applause, and duty. Their inner world shrank to a small, cramped room where there was no space to be weak, needy, or afraid.

In that kind of environment, temptation doesn't just knock politely on the door; it offers an escape hatch. It whispers, "Here is a place where you can feel something other than pressure. Here is a place where you can be wanted, even if it's twisted. Here is a way out."

Again, this is not to justify sin. It is to say that if we only deal with the scandal and never address the years of isolation, overwork, and unprocessed pain that led there, we will keep repeating the same cycle with new names.

Jesus in the Room - The Emmaus Model

When I think about caring for leaders, I often picture Jesus on the road to Emmaus (Luke 24).

Two disciples are walking away from Jerusalem away from the place of pain and disappointment. Their hopes have been crucified. They are confused, disillusioned, and talking it out as they walk.

Jesus joins them.

He doesn't shame them from a distance. He comes alongside them, unrecognised, and asks, "What are you discussing together as you walk along?"

They pour out their confusion. We had hoped they would tell Him exactly how they feel, even though they don't realise they're talking to the risen Christ.

Jesus listens. He asks questions. He lets them tell the truth before He corrects anything.

That, to me, is the heart of a safe space for leaders —Jesus in the room walking with them in their confusion, not rushing to fix them, not punishing their questions, but helping them recognise Him in the middle of their story.

When I sit with a leader, I imagine us on that road. My role is not to be the expert who has all the answers. My role is to create a space where they can say what they had hoped for, and not be punished for it.

Later in the story, Jesus opens the Scriptures and their eyes are opened. But first, He walks, listens, and stays for a meal.

Presence before performance. Companionship before correction.

That is what safe spaces for leaders should feel like.

Pastoral Partnership: A Safe Space to Be Human

Over the years, I've come to call this kind of space **Pastoral Partnership**.[4]

It's a confidential, independent place where leaders, caregivers, and the wounded can tell the truth about what they're carrying and discover that Jesus doesn't walk out of the room.

If you're a leader, you don't have to wait until you're in crisis to seek support. And if you love a leader, you don't have to carry the fear of 'what if they fall,' alone. We can build cultures where care is normal, not exceptional.

My Own Lessons as a Wounded Leader

I don't write this as someone who has always done it well.

There were seasons where I was the one burning out quietly, saying yes when my body was screaming no, carrying everyone else's pain while ignoring my own. I know what it is to lead from an orphan place while hungry for affirmation, terrified of disappointing people, secretly hoping ministry would fill the holes in my heart.

I also know the shame of realising that I had become more comfortable being needed than being loved.

The Fathers outrageous love did not just heal my childhood wounds, it also began to heal my leadership. He invited me to step out of the role of indispensable minister and back into the role of beloved son.

---

[4] "See Pastoral Partnership: Confidential support for leaders, caregivers, and the wounded in the Back Matter."

Part of that healing came through my own safe spaces: spiritual direction, supervision, and trusted friends who were not impressed by my ministry but deeply interested in my heart. People who could look me in the eye and ask, "How are you, really?" and stay long enough to hear the answer.

Those experiences shaped how I now sit with other leaders. I know what it feels like to be the one on the couch, not the one in the chair. I know how much courage it takes to say, I'm not okay, especially when people assume you always are.

A Vision for the Church

I dream of a Church where it is normal, not exceptional, for pastors and leaders to say, "I have a Pastoral Partnership space. I talk to someone about my inner world."

Imagine if:

- Every pastor had a regular, confidential space to process grief, anger, temptation, and fatigue
- Every leadership team budgeted for care the way they budget for sound systems and conferences
- Every denomination and network treated the inner life of leaders as a priority, not an optional extra

Would there still be failures and scandals? Of course. We are human. But I am convinced there would be fewer and that when leaders did stumble, they would have somewhere to fall towards: into the arms of the Father, into communities that know how to restore gently, not just discarded.

Safe spaces for leaders are not a luxury. They are an expression of the Father's heart.

He cares about the sheep. He also cares deeply about the shepherds.

HEART WORK

Reflection, Prayer, and Encounter

Scripture

"Are you tired? Worn out? Burned out on religion? Come to Me. Get away with Me and you'll recover your life. I'll show you how to take a real rest. Walk with Me and work with Me. Watch how I do it. Learn the unforced rhythms of grace."

— Matthew 11:28-29 (The Message)

"Were not our hearts ablaze within us while He was conversing with us on the road, and while he was unveiling the Scriptures to us?"

— Luke 24:32 (Mirror Bible)

Reflection Questions

Choose 1-3 questions that stand out to you today. You don't need to answer them all.

If you're reading in a group, you may choose one question to share and keep the rest private.

- What did you notice about the hidden pressures and vulnerabilities of pastors and leaders?
- How did this chapter affect your view of moral failure and care failure in the Church?
- If you are in any kind of leadership or caregiving role, what are you carrying that you rarely talk about?

- Do you have a truly safe, confidential space to process your inner world? If not, what stops you?

- If you're not in formal leadership, how could you pray for and practically support the leaders in your life?

Journal Prompt

As a leader (or caregiver), the weight I carry that no one sees is __________ and I'm afraid that if I'm honest about it, __________.

Write about the loneliness, the pressure, and the hidden struggles. Then ask Jesus, "Where do You want to meet me in this?" and, "Who is a safe person I can talk to?"

Your Reflections:

One Thing to Try This Week

If you're a leader, reach out to one trusted person (a supervisor, spiritual director, counsellor, or friend) and say, "I need a safe space to process what I'm carrying."

If you're not a leader, text or call one leader in your life and say, "I'm praying for you. How is your heart?"

Breath Prayer for This Week

Inhale: Jesus, You see me

Exhale: I don't have to hide

Let this truth reach the places where you've felt most alone.

Soaking Exercise

Walking the Emmaus Road with Jesus

1. Find a quiet space and invite the Holy Spirit to meet you.

2. Close your eyes and take a few deep breaths. Let yourself settle.

3. Picture yourself walking on a long road. You're tired, confused, maybe grieving or disappointed.

4. Notice that Jesus is walking beside you. He's not rushing you. He's not fixing you. He's just present.

5. He asks, "What are you carrying? What's weighing on your heart?"

6. Tell Him honestly the pressure, the loneliness, the fear, the exhaustion, the questions.

7. Notice how He listens. He doesn't interrupt. He doesn't judge. He's fully present.

8. Ask Him, "What do You want to say to me right now?"

9. Rest in His presence. Let Him be with you in the weight, not just after it's resolved.

What did you notice?

Prayer

Jesus,

You see the weight I carry as a leader (or caregiver).
You see the loneliness, the pressure, the hidden struggles.
You see the parts of me I don't feel safe to show anyone else.

Thank You that You are not disappointed in me.
Thank You that You don't expect me to have it all together.
Thank You that You walk with me not ahead of me or behind me,
but right beside me.

Lead me to safe spaces and safe people, companions, supervisors,
mentors where I can tell the truth and be held as Your beloved child.

Places where I can be honest, where I can process my pain, where I
can be human, not just the leader.

I invite You into my leadership, my ministry, my calling, and my
weariness.
Walk with me on my Emmaus Road.

May I learn how to care for others from a place of being cared for
by You.
Thank You that You are always in the room, even when I feel most
alone.

Heal the parts of me that believe I have to carry it all alone.
May I learn the unforced rhythms of grace.

I don't have to hide anymore.
You are in the room.

Let it be so.

Amen.

HEART KEYS FOR LEADERS – CARING FOR THE CAREGIVERS

Who Cares for the Caregivers?

Over the years, I've become deeply passionate about heart healing for leaders — not because leaders are worse than anyone else, but because the stakes are higher when a leader's pain goes unattended.

Ministry can be lonely. You're expected to carry others, stay strong, and keep showing up. People come to you when their world is falling apart. They tell you the stories they've never told anyone. They ask you to pray, to counsel, to lead, to decide, to hold.

And yet many leaders have no truly safe place to be honest about what's happening inside.

That's where pastoral partnership (supervision) has been a gift in my own life — and why I believe it's part of how we prevent crisis, not just respond to it.

Pastoral partnership is a confidential, structured space — ideally independent of your church's power dynamics — where leaders can process their inner world, reflect on ministry practice, and receive support and accountability without fear of gossip or instant consequences.[5]

---

[5] "See Pastoral Partnership: Confidential support for leaders, caregivers, and the wounded in the Back Matter."

I wouldn't be where I am today without it.

After **School of Ministry**, after stepping into inner healing ministry, after launching **Heart Keys**, I knew I needed support. I couldn't carry the weight of other people's stories without someone helping me carry mine. Pastoral partnership gave me space to stay grounded in my identity as a son, to notice what was happening in my own heart, and to remember that I'm human — not just 'the minister.'

A Mega-Church Pastor on the Edge

One of the most sobering journeys I've walked has been with a mega-church pastor.

He led a large church with more than a dozen campuses internationally. Thousands of people. Global invitations. A public profile that looked, from the outside, like the pinnacle of ministry in his forties.

And then came what the Church often calls a 'moral failure.'

I don't minimise sin or its impact. Choices matter. Boundaries matter. Accountability matters. Real people get hurt when leaders' cross lines.

But as I walked with him, I also saw something deeper: a heart crying out for love, attention, and comfort — places in him that had never learned how to receive care without performing for it.

When you're carrying that level of responsibility and visibility, the weight is immense. If past hurts, family-of-origin pain, and unmet needs haven't been tended to, cracks eventually appear. Not always on the outside at first — often in the private places where no one is watching.

In the middle of what looked like success, his inner world was collapsing.

And yet, even there, the kindness of God was at work.

Scripture says it's His kindness that leads us to repentance — not fear, not shame, not the terror of being exposed. In the middle of everything, there was a moment that changed the trajectory of his healing.

He prayed, "God, would You father me?"

There was a pause.

Then, deep in his spirit, he sensed the Holy Spirit ask:

"Are you sure you want God to father you?"

That's not a light question.

To be fathered by God means allowing Him into places we've kept tightly controlled. It means letting Him dismantle the survival structures we built to cope. It means surrendering the false strength that looks impressive but leaves us alone.

After a moment, he asked again, "Yes. God — will You father me?"

In that yes, something began to unravel — not in a destructive way, but in a redemptive way. The Father's love started reaching places in him that had never experienced unconditional compassion or comfort.

When real love comes close, it often reveals the places in us that don't yet feel lovable.

And sometimes, out of those unhealed places, we respond in unhealthy ways.

That's what had happened for this apostolic leader.

But the story didn't end there.

Over two years, I watched the Father walk him through a deep journey of heart healing. I watched Jesus meet him in his darkest moments — not just as King, but as Healer and Comforter. I watched the Holy Spirit gently expose lies, heal experiences, and restore identity, one day at a time.

His decisions had real consequences for him, his family, his church, and thousands of people.

And yet, in the middle of that, I watched God restore him — slowly, patiently, faithfully.

Today, he's on the other side of that initial collapse. He is still on the journey, still learning, still in process, but moving forward again.

And I believe the Father's word over him is not a sentence of shame, but a call back into sonship:

"This is My son, whom I love."

Not because he never failed.

But because he allowed God to father him in the middle of his failure.

When the System Fails: A Convicted Priest

Another significant moment that shaped my heart for leaders goes back to my younger years in the inner-city Melbourne parish where I grew up.

I was an altar boy there. I loved serving in the house of God. But even as a kid, I remember a cloud of suspicion around one of our parish priests — whispers about his history in other parishes, things people didn't say outright but hinted at.

In time, he was removed from the parish.

Eventually, it came out that he had abused children in previous churches. He was convicted of child abuse and molestation and went to jail.

I'm grateful I was never abused by him and never felt at risk in his presence.

But my heart is deeply empathetic toward those who were harmed — their pain, their trauma, their stolen innocence.

Years later, after his release from jail, I had the opportunity to visit him where he was living.

I remember sitting with him one afternoon, listening to his story.

He didn't deny the abuse. He didn't excuse what he had done.

And as I listened, I began to see a wider context — not to minimise the harm, but to understand how a life can become so broken and twisted.

He grew up in a highly performance-based environment, in a family where everyone was a doctor. He didn't have the capacity to follow that path, and he never felt like he measured up. From a young age he wrestled with same-sex attraction at a time when there was virtually no safe space in the Church to talk about it.

Back then, for a young Catholic man, the options felt brutally simple: get married or enter holy orders.

There was no language for orientation, no place to bring shame and confusion into the light, no permission to be honest about what was happening inside.

So he did what he thought was the 'holy' thing. He joined the seminary, became a priest, and tried to outrun or suppress parts of himself he didn't understand.

He'd been sent to boarding school as a boy, with very little nurture or connection. He learned early how to perform, how to comply, and how to keep things hidden.

Again, none of this excuses his actions.

But it does paint a picture: a man with deep unmet needs, no safe place to process them, and a system that rewarded silence and appearance.

He was also formed in communities where secrecy had already normalised what was profoundly destructive. When broken men cluster together in hiddenness, they begin to treat the abnormal as normal.

And young lives pay the price.

Sitting with him, I felt the weight of both realities: the devastating harm he had caused; and the devastating lack of nurture, support, and honest spaces in his own formation.

His story highlighted something for me: Leaders — priests, pastors, ministers — need more than a title and a collar. They need robust, holistic spaces where they can bring their full internal world: their temptations and confusion; their loneliness and isolation; their trauma, family-of-origin pain, and unmet needs.

Spaces where they can be vulnerable without fear of losing everything. Spaces where they can be seen, loved, and challenged before their pain turns into harm.

Spiritual direction is beautiful and vital. It helps us recognise God's presence in the now-tense of our lives.

But when someone's body, soul, and emotions are crying out — when there are deep questions around sexuality, identity, shame, and unmet needs — spiritual direction may not be enough on its own.

Sometimes we also need supervision, wise community, practical safeguards, and professional support to help us carry what we're carrying.

A Gentle Invitation to Leaders

If you're a leader reading this, I want you to hear this clearly:

You are allowed to need care. You are allowed to have limits. You are allowed to be in process.

Getting support isn't a sign you're failing. It's a sign you're human.

And it may be one of the kindest things you do — not only for your own heart, but for the people you lead.

If you want a picture of what I mean, go back to the Emmaus Road in Luke 24 — Jesus walking with the disillusioned, listening before correcting. Presence before performance. Companionship before correction.

That is what safe spaces for leaders are meant to feel like.

HEART WORK

Reflection, Prayer, and Encounter

Scripture

"The Lord is my best friend and my shepherd. I always have more than enough. He offers a resting place for me in his luxurious love. His tracks take me to an oasis of peace, the quiet brook of bliss."

— Psalm 23:1–2 (TPT)

"God, my shepherd! I don't need a thing. You have bedded me down in lush meadows, you find me quiet pools to drink from. True to your word, you let me catch my breath and send me in the right direction."

— Psalm 23:1–3 (The Message)

Reflection Questions

Choose 1–3 questions that stand out to you today., You don't need to answer them all.

If you're reading in a group, you may choose one question to share and keep the rest private.

- As a leader or caregiver, where are you carrying more than you can honestly hold?

- Do you have access to pastoral supervision, spiritual direction, or another structured support? If not, what would it take to pursue that?

- Which parts of the mega-church pastor's story or the priest's story resonated with you — not in behaviour, but in unmet needs or isolation?

- Have you ever felt unable to be vulnerable because of your role? What has that cost you?

- What's one step you could take toward getting support — pastoral supervision, inner healing, or another safe space?

Journal Prompt

"If I'm honest, the part of leadership that is costing me the most is… and I've been afraid to admit it because…"

Write about the hidden cost, the toll on your marriage, your health, your heart, your faith. Then ask the Father, "What do You want to say to me about this? What support do You want me to receive?"

Your Reflections:

One Thing to Try This Week

Research one form of support: pastoral supervision, spiritual direction, counselling, or a peer support group for leaders. Make one phone call, send one email, or visit one website. Take the first step toward not carrying it alone.

Breath Prayer for This Week

Inhale: "I am a son/daughter first"
Exhale: "Not a ministry machine"

Let this truth quiet the voice that says your worth is in your output.

Soaking Exercise
Resting in the Shepherd's Care

1. Find a quiet, comfortable space. Invite the Holy Spirit to lead you.

2. Close your eyes and take a few deep breaths. Let your body relax.

3. Picture yourself as a sheep lying down in green pastures beside still waters. You're not leading anyone. You're not responsible for anyone. You're simply being cared for.

4. Notice: The Shepherd (Jesus) is with you. He's not asking you to do anything. He's simply tending to you.

5. Ask Him, "What part of me needs Your care right now?" Let Him show you, your exhaustion, your loneliness, your wounds, your unmet needs.

6. Let Him care for you. Maybe He's speaking, maybe He's silent, maybe He's just sitting with you. Receive whatever He offers.

7. Ask Him, "What would it look like for me to let others care for me the way You're caring for me now?"

8. Rest as long as you need. When you're ready, thank Him for being your Shepherd, not your taskmaster.

What did you notice?

Prayer

Father,
I confess I've been running on empty.
I've been giving from a place of depletion, not overflow.
I've believed that rest is weakness,
that asking for help is failure,
that I have to hold it all together for everyone else.

Forgive me for treating myself like a ministry machine
instead of Your beloved child.

Lead me to safe, structured support,
supervision, direction, counselling, community.
Give me courage to be honest about what I'm carrying.
Heal the unmet needs beneath my ministry.

May I learn to lead from rest, not exhaustion.
May I learn to care for others from a full heart, not an empty one.

I am Your sheep.
You are my Shepherd.
I don't have to carry it all alone.

Let it be so.

Amen.

PART V

THE INVITATION AND THE FRUIT

PREFACE

By the time you reach Part V, you've walked through some of the most tender terrain of my story: the early wounding, the long search for belonging, the Father's relentless pursuit, and the practical ways healing has taken shape — both in my own life and in the lives of others.

But I don't want this book to end as something you simply read about.

Part V is where the story becomes an invitation.

Because the deepest hope of Outrageous Love is not that you would admire a testimony, or learn a few new ideas about healing. It's that you would awaken and encounter the Father for yourself — right where you are, in your real life, with your real story.

Healing is rarely instant, and it's almost never tidy. Often it looks like small, faithful steps: telling the truth, letting yourself be seen, receiving comfort, choosing forgiveness when you're ready, learning new boundaries, and discovering that God is present in the places you once believed were too broken to hold Him.

In this final part, I want to hold out a simple possibility: what if the love that met me is reaching for you, too?

If you're carrying shame, I want you to know you don't have to earn your way back. If you're tired, I want you to know you don't have to strive to be held. If you feel stuck, I want you to know the Father is not impatient with your process.

And if you're a leader or caregiver, I want you to know the fruit of healing is not just personal peace — it's generational. One healed heart really can change families, communities, and the way we lead.

So as you enter Part V, I invite you to slow down again. Let the words become prayer. Let the memories that surface be met with gentleness. And if you need to pause, do that. The Holy Spirit is not in a hurry.

My prayer is that you won't just finish this book — you'll find yourself more deeply at home in the Father's love.

Welcome to the invitation. And welcome to the fruit.

CHAPTER 13

THE INVITATION

He Never Turned Away

By now, you've heard a lot of my story.

The little boy playing 'Pope' in the backyard. The teenager searching in the darkness. The drag queen who thought he'd gone too far. The man undone by the Father's love. The son learning to receive, to rest, and to live from belovedness.

If there's one thread running through it all, it's this:

He never turned away. Not once.

Not when I was abused. Not when I was numbing myself in clubs and substances. Not when I was performing and pretending. Not when I was angry, confused, or ashamed. Not when I was trying to fix myself.

He never turned away.

And He hasn't turned away from you either.

This Story Is Also About You

It might be tempting to read my story like a movie: "That's powerful, Lawrence. What a testimony. God really did a work in you."

And then close the book and go back to life as usual.

But *Outrageous Love* was never meant to be just my story.

It's meant to awaken you to your story with the Father. Because the same love that met me in my mess is reaching for you in yours — right now, in your context, in your real life, with your real questions.

This isn't just a testimony. It's an invitation.

Come Home (Not Try Harder)

Along the way, we've talked about the orphan mindset and the journey into sonship.

Maybe you recognised yourself in some of the orphan patterns: feeling like you're never enough; striving to earn love, approval, or belonging; living in comparison or fear of being exposed; carrying a low-grade shame that never quite lifts.

Or maybe you saw yourself in the stories of leaders: carrying more than you can honestly hold; feeling lonely, pressured, and responsible for everyone else; afraid to be vulnerable because of your role.

Wherever you find yourself, the Father's heart toward you is the same:

"You are My beloved. You are not alone. You don't have to strive. Come home."

The invitation is not to try harder. It's to come home to love.

You Don't Have to Fix Yourself First

One of the biggest lies I believed for years was: "When I clean myself up, then I can come to God."

So I tried. I tried to be holy enough, disciplined enough, spiritual enough.

It never worked.

Because the gospel is not 'fix yourself and then come.' The gospel is 'come as you are, and I will heal you from the inside out.'

Jesus didn't wait for the woman at the well to get her life together before He met her. He didn't wait for Peter to stop failing before He restored him. He didn't wait for me to become respectable before He came close.

He comes into our reality and meets us there.

Letting Him Into the Deep Places

For some of you, the next step is to let Him into the places you've never let anyone see: the memories you've pushed down; the abuse, betrayal, or abandonment you've never really processed; the shame you've carried for years; the vows you've made such as, "I'll never trust again," "I'll never be vulnerable, " or, "I'll never need anyone."

He's not afraid of those places. He already sees them. And He loves you there.

Inner healing isn't about digging endlessly for pain. It's about inviting Jesus into the moments that shaped you so He can show you where He was, what He says, and who you are.

And you don't have to do it alone. You may need a safe person — a prayer minister, counsellor, spiritual director, supervisor, or trusted friend — to walk with you.[6]

That's not weakness. That's wisdom.

---

[6] "See Pastoral Partnership: Confidential support for leaders, caregivers, and the wounded in the Back Matter."

A Word for Leaders and Caregivers

If you're a pastor, priest, leader, or caregiver, I want to speak to you directly.

You are not a machine. You are not a ministry robot. You are a beloved son or daughter.

You are allowed to have needs. You are allowed to be tired. You are allowed to be human.

You don't have to wait for a crisis to get help.[7] If something in the stories of leaders stirred something in you — loneliness, pressure, unmet needs — please don't ignore that. It may be the kindness of God inviting you into deeper care before something breaks.

The Father's Heart for You

If I could sit across from you right now, look you in the eyes, and say one thing, it would be this:

You are not too far gone. You are not too broken. You are not too much. You are not disqualified from love.

The Father is not rolling His eyes at you. He's not waiting for you to get it together.

He's running down the road like the father in Luke 15 — robe flying, arms wide, eyes full of joy — saying, "My child is coming home."

He's not interested in making you a better orphan. He wants to restore you as a son or daughter.

---

[7] "See Pastoral Partnership: in the Back Matter."

A Simple Prayer of Response

You can use this prayer as a starting point — in your own words, at your own pace.

Father, I come to You just as I am — with my story, my wounds, my shame, my questions, and my desires. I'm tired of trying to fix myself. I'm tired of striving, performing, and pretending.

I want to know You as You really are. I want to know You as Father. I want to know Jesus as my Healer, my Saviour, my Friend. I want to know the Holy Spirit as my Comforter and Guide.

I invite You into my heart, into my memories, into my beliefs about myself and about You. Show me where You were in my pain. Speak truth over the lies I've believed.

I choose to forgive those who have wounded me — not because they deserve it, but because I want to be free. I choose to release them into Your hands.

Restore me to my original design. Heal my heart from the inside out. Teach me to live as Your beloved, not as an orphan.

I say yes to Your outrageous love. Let it be so. Amen.

Stepping Into the Journey

Healing is a journey. There are moments of awakening and encounter that change everything in an instant. And there are long, slow seasons where the Father patiently walks with us, layer by layer.

Don't despise the process. Don't compare your journey to someone else's. Don't assume that because you still feel pain, God isn't working.

He is.

Sometimes the most powerful thing you can do is simply keep showing up; keep bringing your heart to Him; keep asking, "Father, what do You say about this?"; keep inviting Jesus into what surfaces; keep letting the Holy Spirit lead you into truth

You don't walk this road alone.

As you close this chapter, I want you to know that your story matters. Your heart matters.

And the love that met me is reaching for you too.

HEART WORK

Reflection, Prayer, and Encounter

Scripture

"When the son was still a long way off, his father saw him coming and was filled with loving compassion. He ran to him, embraced him, and kissed him over and over!"

— Luke 15:20 (TPT)

"When he was still a long way off, his father saw him. His heart pounding, he ran out, embraced him, and kissed him."

— Luke 15:20 (The Message)

Reflection Questions

Choose 1-3 questions that stand out to you today. You don't need to answer them all.

If you're reading in a group, you may choose one question to share and keep the rest private.

- Where did you most clearly see your own story reflected in my journey?
- What is currently holding you back from fully receiving the Father's love?
- What lie about God or about yourself do you sense the Father inviting you to renounce today?
- Can you imagine the Father running toward you with open arms? What emotions does that stir up?

- What would it look like, in practical terms, for you to "come home" in this season?

Journal Prompt

"If I said yes to the Father's love today, the first thing that would change in my life is…"

Write honestly about what's holding you back and what might shift if you truly believed you were beloved. Then ask the Father, "What are You inviting me into?"

Your Reflections:

One Thing to Try This Week

Pray the 'Simple Prayer of Response' from this chapter out loud — in your own words, at your own pace. Don't rush it. Let it be a real conversation with the Father, not a formula.

Breath Prayer for This Week

Inhale: "I am coming home"
Exhale: "You never turned away"

Let this truth settle deeper than every wound, every shame, every fear.

Soaking Exercise

The Father Running Toward You

1. Find a quiet, safe space. Invite the Holy Spirit to meet you here.

2. Close your eyes and take a few deep breaths. Let yourself settle.

3. Picture yourself on a road, walking toward home. You're tired, maybe ashamed, maybe hopeful, maybe afraid.

4. In the distance, you see the Father. He sees you.

5. Notice: He doesn't wait. He doesn't cross His arms. He runs toward you — robe flying, arms wide, tears in His eyes.

6. Let yourself feel whatever comes — relief, disbelief, resistance, longing, fear, joy.

7. He reaches you. He embraces you. Ask Him, "What do You want to say to me?"

8. Listen. Receive. Let Him speak identity, love, and welcome over you.

9. Rest in His embrace as long as you need. You are home.

What did you notice?

Prayer

Father,
I come to You just as I am,
with my story, my wounds, my shame, my questions, and my desires.

I'm tired of trying to fix myself.
I'm tired of striving, performing, and pretending.

I want to know You as You really are.
I want to know You as Father.
I want to know Jesus as my healer, my Saviour, my friend.
I want to know the Holy Spirit as my comforter and guide.

I invite You into my heart,
into my memories,
into my beliefs about myself and about You.

Show me where You were in my pain.
Speak truth over the lies I've believed.

I choose to forgive those who have wounded me —
not because they deserve it,
but because I want to be free.
I choose to release them into Your hands.

Restore me to my original design.
Heal my heart from the inside out.
May I learn to live as Your beloved, not as an orphan.

I say yes to Your outrageous love.

Let it be so.

Amen.

THE FRUIT OF HEALING

Not a Finished Product, but a Different Man

If you've made it this far, you might be expecting a neat, tidy ending. "Lawrence got healed, everything worked out, the credits rolled, and he never struggled again."

That's not my story.

I'm not a finished product. I still have days where old lies whisper. I still have moments where the orphan mindset tries to creep back in. I still need supervision, spiritual direction, inner healing, community[8] — and the daily reminder: I am the Father's beloved son.

But I am not the man I used to be.

And that, to me, is the fruit of healing.

What's Different Now

Here's what's changed — not in theory, but in the lived reality of my life:

---

[8] "See Pastoral Partnership: Confidential support for leaders, caregivers, and the wounded in the Back Matter."

- **Love is no longer just an idea.**

  I know I am loved — not as a concept, but as a growing, felt reality. The Father's love has moved from my head to my heart.

- **Shame no longer defines me.**

  The abuse, the clubs, the drag persona, the drug world — they're part of my story, but they're not my identity. I can speak about them without drowning in shame.

- **I live from sonship, not striving.**

  I still work hard, but I'm no longer trying to earn love or prove my worth. I work with the Father, not for Him as an anxious employee.

- **My relationships are healthier.**

  I can set boundaries. I can say no. I can apologise. I can receive love without constantly waiting for it to be taken away.

- **I'm more present to my own heart.**

  Instead of numbing, I notice what's going on inside. I bring it to God. I talk about it with safe people. I don't have to hide.

- **I get to partner with the Trinity in others' healing.**

  Through **Heart Keys** and **Professional Pastoral Partnership**, I've watched the Father heal hearts, restore identities, and help leaders who thought they were done.

None of this is because I'm impressive. It's because His love is.

The Ripple Effect

I've watched the fruit of healing ripple out in ways I never could have orchestrated: - families breaking generational patterns of abuse, addiction, and silence - men and women who thought they were "too far gone" discovering they are deeply loved and wanted - leaders on the brink of burnout finding safe spaces to process, heal, and stay in the race in a healthier way - people who once hid in shame now becoming safe places for others.

I've seen Jesus show up in memories, in living rooms, in Zoom calls, in conference halls, and in quiet moments of surrender.

I've watched people realise — often with tears:

"He was there. He never turned away from me either."

That's the fruit of healing. Not perfection. Presence.

Your Story Continues

As you close this book, your story is still being written.

There will be days when you feel the Father's love strongly, and days when you feel nothing. There will be moments of breakthrough and moments of slow, hidden faithfulness. There will be times when old patterns knock on the door.

None of that disqualifies you.

The invitation is the same, day after day: Keep coming back to the Father's embrace. Keep choosing truth over the lie. Keep letting yourself be loved.

And when you need help, reach for it. Healing multiplies in safe spaces.

One Healed Heart

One healed heart can change a family. One healed heart can change a community. One healed heart can change a generation.

May that healed heart be yours.

Nothing can separate you from the love of God. Not your past. Not your pain. Not your questions. Not your process.

He never turned away. And He never will.

HEART WORK

Reflection, Prayer, and Encounter

Scripture

"I am convinced that nothing can ever separate us from God's love. Neither death nor life, neither angels nor demons, neither our fears for today nor our worries about tomorrow — not even the powers of hell can separate us from God's love."

— Romans 8:38 (NLT)

"So now I live with the confidence that there is nothing in the universe with the power to separate us from God's love. I'm convinced that his love will triumph over death, life's troubles, fallen angels, or dark rulers in the heavens. There is nothing in our present or future circumstances that can weaken his love."

— Romans 8:38 (TPT)

"There is nothing that can separate us from the love of God."

— Romans 8:39 (Mirror Bible)

Reflection Questions

Choose 1–3 questions that stand out to you today, you don't need to answer them all.

If you're reading in a group, you may choose one question to share and keep the rest private.

- Looking at your own story, what generational cycles or patterns is God inviting you to break?

- How can you "father" or "mother" the next generation — biologically or spiritually — out of healing rather than out of your wounds?

- Where have you been relating to others (or leading) from fear instead of love?

- What would it look like to release control and trust the Father with your story and your future?

- If your heart continues to heal, what kind of legacy do you hope to leave for the next generation?

Journal Prompt

"The fruit of healing I most long to see in my life is... and the ripple effect I hope it has is..."

Write about the transformation you're longing for — not just for yourself, but for your family, your community, the next generation. Then ask the Father, "What are You already doing that I haven't noticed yet?"

Your Reflections:

One Thing to Try This Week

Write down one generational pattern you want to break (e.g., silence around pain, performance-based love, fear of vulnerability). Declare out loud, "This pattern stops with me. I choose healing, honesty, and love for the next generation."

Breath Prayer for This Week

Inhale: "One healed heart"
Exhale: "Can change a generation"

Let this truth fuel your courage to keep walking the healing journey.

Soaking Exercise
Seeing the Ripple Effect

1. Find a quiet space and invite the Holy Spirit to give you His perspective.
2. Close your eyes and take a few deep breaths. Let yourself settle.
3. Picture a still pond. You drop a stone into the water. Watch the ripples spread outward, wider and wider, farther than you can see.
4. Ask the Father, "What is the fruit of my healing? Where are the ripples going?"
5. Let Him show you, your children, your friends, your community, people you haven't even met yet.
6. Notice: Your healing is not just for you. It's for them.
7. Ask Him, "What legacy do You want me to leave? What would it look like to live from healed love, not wounded fear?"
8. Rest in His vision for your life. Let it anchor you in the ongoing journey.

What did you notice?

Prayer

Father,
Thank You for the journey of healing,
the breakthroughs and the slow, hidden work.

I'm not finished with my life yet, but I'm not the person I used to be.
And that is the fruit of Your love.

I ask You now:
Break the generational cycles of pain in my family.
Let healing begin with me.

May I learn to father and mother others,
biologically and spiritually,
out of wholeness, not woundedness.

Help me to lead and love from rest, not fear.
Help me to trust You with my story and my future.

May my healed heart be a ripple that spreads,
to my family, my community, and generations I'll never meet.

One healed heart can change a family.
One healed heart can change a community.
One healed heart can change a generation.

Let that healed heart be mine.

Thank You that nothing can separate me from Your love,
not my past, not my mistakes, not my wounds.

You never turned away.
And You never will.

Amen.

HOW TO USE THIS BOOK IN A GROUP

This book is designed to be read slowly, honestly, and together. The goal isn't to get through all the content as quickly as possible, but to create safe spaces where people can encounter the Father's love and begin (or continue) their own healing journey.

You can use this book in: small groups or home groups, book clubs, recovery or support groups, leadership teams, one-on-one mentoring or spiritual direction

1. Create a Safe Space

Before anything else, agree together on:

- Confidentiality — What's shared here stays here.
- No fixing — You're not here to rescue, diagnose, or correct one another.
- No pressure — People can share as much or as little as they want. Passing is always allowed.
- Honour — Listen without interrupting, mocking, or minimising anyone's story.

You might want to open each meeting with a simple prayer inviting the Holy Spirit to lead, comfort, and protect.

2. Suggested Rhythm

1. Read

Either read the chapter in advance, or read key sections aloud together (especially the stories).

2. Reflect

Take a few quiet minutes for personal reflection before discussion. Invite people to write down what stood out, what stirred them, or where they felt resistance.

3. Share

Use the Heart Work questions as a guide, not a checklist. Pick questions that feel most relevant to your group. Let conversation flow naturally; you don't have to answer everything.

4. Respond

Close with a simple response: a time of silent prayer, use the closing prayer from the Heart Work section, or invite people to ask Jesus a question (e.g., "Where were You in this memory?"). If appropriate, you can pray gently for one another in pairs or as a group.

5. Optional: Practise Together

If your group is comfortable, you could do one of the Heart Work exercises together — such as the Soaking Exercise or Breath Prayer — before closing. This models vulnerability and gives people permission to engage.

3. Tips for Group Leaders

- Model vulnerability. Share from your own story first. Your honesty will give others permission to be real.
- Watch the clock, but don't rush the heart. It's better to go deep on one question than skim ten.

- Respect emotional capacity. Some chapters may touch trauma. If strong emotions surface, slow down, ground the person (breathing, present-moment awareness), and don't force them to share details.

- Know your limits. This book is not a substitute for professional counselling or therapy. If someone discloses serious abuse, self-harm, or danger, gently encourage them to seek appropriate help and follow your church/organisation's safeguarding policies.

- Encourage the Heart Work exercises. Remind participants that the journaling prompts, breath prayers, and soaking exercises are designed to help them encounter God personally, not just talk about Him.

4. For Leadership Teams

If you're using this book with pastors, priests, or ministry leaders:

- Pay special attention to Chapters 11 and 12.
- Consider building in extra time for processing and prayer around burnout, shame, and the need for supervision and support.
- Make it clear that this is not an evaluation space, but a care space.

5. Go at the Pace of Grace

Some groups will move through a chapter a week. Others may spend several weeks on a single section that hits close to home. That's okay.

The aim is not to 'finish the book.' The aim is to let the Father's outrageous love sink from the page into your hearts, one layer at a time.

6. Using the Heart Work Sections in Groups

Each chapter's Heart Work section is designed primarily for personal reflection, but you can adapt elements for group use:

- Reflection Questions: Use 3–5 questions as discussion starters.
- Journal Prompt: Invite participants to write silently for 5 minutes, then share one sentence or insight if they're comfortable.
- One Thing to Try This Week: Encourage participants to commit to one practice and check in next session.
- Breath Prayer: Practise it together at the end of your meeting.
- Soaking Exercise: If your group is comfortable with contemplative prayer, guide them through the exercise together (10–15 minutes of silence with gentle prompts).
- Closing Prayer: Read the prayer aloud together, or invite someone to pray it over the group.

DISCUSSION QUESTIONS

For Personal Reflection or Group Study

These questions are designed to help you process the themes of this book, encounter the Father's love for yourself, and apply the truths to your own journey.

If any question feels too tender, you're free to skip it and come back later. Go at the pace of grace.

Chapter 1: The Little Pope

- What was your first encounter with God's presence? How did it shape your understanding of who He is?

- Where do you see God's fingerprints in your childhood, even in moments you didn't recognise Him at the time?

- What does 'childlike faith' look like for you today? Where have you lost that simplicity?

- What hunger has God planted in your heart? Is it still alive, or has it been buried?

- Can you identify a time when God was pursuing you, even when you didn't realise it?

Chapter 2: When Fathers Leave

- How has your relationship with your earthly father (or lack thereof) shaped your view of God the Father?

- What lies have you believed about God because of wounds from your past?
- Do you sense you might be carrying a prenatal or early-life wound? What lie might have been planted there?
- Have you experienced sexual abuse or molestation? Have you ever spoken about it in a safe space?
- What lies have you believed about yourself because of abuse or trauma?
- What generational patterns or cycles of pain can you see in your family story?
- Can you look at your parent(s) with compassion, recognising the wounds they carried?
- What generational cycle is God inviting you to break?

Chapter 3: Searching in the Darkness

- Where have you searched for identity, love, and belonging outside of God?
- What "false selves" or personas have you created to feel accepted?
- Have you ever felt like you had to perform to be loved? Where did that belief come from?
- What does it mean to you that Jesus was present in your darkest moments, not condemning but loving?
- How do you respond to the idea that feelings and emotions matter in the context of sexuality and identity?
- Have you drawn lines that Jesus is inviting you to cross — people you've excluded or judged?
- How well have you loved? Not "How right have you been?", but "How well have you loved?"

Chapter 4: The Twelve-Year Journey

- Where have you experienced God's patience in your life? How long has He been waiting for you?

- Have you ever felt like you were 'doing Christianity wrong' because transformation wasn't happening fast enough?

- Who in your life has loved you unconditionally, without rushing to correct or fix you?

- Are you waiting for 'the axe to fall' in any relationship — with God or with people?

- What would it look like to see the process itself as part of God's goodness, rather than demanding instant change?

Chapter 5: The Father's Love

- What lies have you believed about God the Father because of your earthly father or other authority figures?

- Can you imagine the Father loving you as much as He loves Jesus? What makes that hard to believe?

- Where do you need the Father to show up and heal the father wound in your heart?

- Have you believed the lie that 'God can't look upon sin?' How has that shaped your relationship with Him?

- What would it look like to let the Father reintroduce Himself to you?

Chapter 6: Learning to Receive

- Do you know how to receive love, or do you mostly know how to give it?

- What makes it hard for you to receive — from God or from others? Where does that resistance come from?

- Have you ever felt like you were 'wasting time' by just resting in God's presence?

- What might it look like for you to practise soaking in God's love in the next season?

- Are you running on empty, constantly giving but rarely being filled? What needs to change?

Chapter 7: From Orphan to Son

- Do you operate more as an orphan or as a son/daughter? What evidence do you see in your life?

- Which orphan tendencies (striving, comparison, fear of rejection, self-protection) do you recognise in yourself?

- Can you believe that the Father has never changed His mind about you? Why or why not?

- What would it look like for you to shift from performing to resting?

- How would your life change if you fully believed you were a beloved son or daughter?

Chapter 8: Prophetic Leaking

- Have you ever experienced 'prophetic leaking' — where God's heart for someone just overflowed out of you? What happened?

- What deep beliefs about your identity might you need to ask God about, like I did with "Am I gay?"

- Have you ever gotten a prophetic word wrong or shared something prematurely? How did you respond?

- Are you operating in the prophetic from rest and sonship, or from a need for approval and significance?

- What would it look like for you to only say what God asks you to say, and to keep the rest for prayer?

Chapter 9: Heart Keys — Healing from the Inside Out

- What wounds are you carrying that need the Father's healing touch?

- Have you ever invited Jesus into a painful memory? What happened — or what do you fear might happen?

- Who do you need to forgive? What is holding you back from releasing them?

- Where do you see 'braided' patterns like rejection/abandonment/loss and anger/fear/grief in your own story?

- What lies have you believed about yourself because of past wounds?

- What would it look like for you to be restored to your original design?

Chapter 10: Stories from the Healing Room

- Which story in this chapter resonated with you most — Emma, Daniel, Mark, or another? Why?

- Where do you see similar patterns in your own life (e.g., fear of abandonment, using comfort to numb pain, burnout)?

- If Jesus stepped into one of your painful memories today, what do you imagine He might do or say?

- Are there inner vows you've made ("I'll never trust again," or "I have to do it all myself") that God is inviting you to revisit?

- Who is one safe person you could invite into your healing journey?

Chapter 11: Safe Spaces for Leaders — Jesus in the Room

- What did you learn about the hidden pressures and vulnerabilities of pastors and leaders?

- How did the stories of leaders in this book affect your view of 'moral failure' and '"care failure' in the Church?

- If you are in any kind of leadership or caregiving role, what are you carrying that you rarely talk about?

- Do you have a truly safe, confidential space to process your inner world? If not, what stops you?

- If you're not in formal leadership, how could you pray for and practically support the leaders in your life?

Chapter 12: Heart Keys for Leaders — Caring for the Caregivers

- As a leader or caregiver, where are you carrying more than you can honestly hold?

- Do you have access to pastoral supervision, spiritual direction, or another structured support? If not, what would it take to pursue that?

- Which parts of the megachurch pastor's story or the priest's story resonated with you — not in behaviour, but in unmet needs or isolation?

- Have you ever felt unable to be vulnerable because of your role? What has that cost you?

- What's one step you could take toward getting support — pastoral supervision, inner healing, or another safe space?

Chapter 13: The Invitation

- Where did you most clearly see your own story reflected in my journey?

- What is currently holding you back from fully receiving the Father's love?

- What lie about God or about yourself do you sense the Father inviting you to renounce today?

- Can you imagine the Father running toward you with open arms? What emotions does that stir up?

- What would it look like, in practical terms, for you to 'come home' in this season?

Epilogue: The Fruit of Healing

- Looking at your own story, what generational cycles or patterns is God inviting you to break?

- How can you "father" or "mother" the next generation — biologically or spiritually — out of healing rather than out of your wounds?

- Where have you been relating to others (or leading) from fear instead of love?

- What would it look like to release control and trust the Father with your story and your future?

- If your heart continues to heal, what kind of legacy do you hope to leave for the next generation?

Whole Book — Going Deeper

1. Looking back over the whole book, what is one lie about God and one lie about yourself that have been most challenged?

2. Where do you sense the Father inviting you into a deeper journey of healing — identity, memories, relationships, leadership, or something else?

3. Who in your life might need to hear a story like this? How could you share your own journey with them in a way that is honest and safe?

4. What practices (soaking, journaling, Examen, supervision, inner healing prayer, community) do you want to intentionally build into your life as a result of reading this book?

5. If you could summarise what you're taking away from this book in one sentence, what would it be?

PASTORAL PARTNERSHIP

Confidential support for leaders, caregivers, and the wounded

What Pastoral Partnership Is

Pastoral Partnership is a confidential, independent space where you can bring your inner world into the light — without needing to perform, explain it away, or rush back to being fine.

It's a place to, tell the truth about what you're carrying, notice what's happening in your body (not just your theology), listen for Jesus in the middle of your story, receive care, not just give it, and grow in wholeness, integrity, and sustainable leadership.

*In the USA and Canada, this kind of support is offered through **Professional Pastoral Partnership***

What Pastoral Partnership Is Not

Pastoral Partnership is no, a gossip session about your church or team, a secret club that undermines accountability, a place to rehearse self-pity with no invitation to growth, nor a replacement for professional mental health care when that's what you need.

How It's Different (Simple Guide)

Support type	Primary focus	What it often includes	Best when you need
Pastoral Partnership (pastoral supervision)	Your inner life, leadership pressures, calling, integrity, and sustainability	Confidential conversation, reflection, prayerful attentiveness, healthy boundaries, trauma-aware insight	A safe space to process leadership weight, temptation, fatigue, conflict, grief, and identity beyond the role
Spiritual Direction	Your relationship with God and spiritual formation	Listening prayer, discernment, noticing God's movements, practices	Help hearing God, deepening prayer, integrating faith and life
Counselling / Therapy	Mental health, trauma, patterns, and healing	Evidence-based therapeutic approaches, diagnosis (sometimes), treatment plans	Trauma recovery, anxiety/depression, relational patterns, significant distress
Mentoring / Coaching	Skills, goals, strategy, and development	Advice, frameworks, accountability, action plans	Practical growth, leadership skills, decision-making, next steps

Note: These can overlap. The key is knowing what you're asking for and choosing a space that is safe, trauma-aware, and appropriately qualified.

What a Safe Space Should Feel Like

A safe space is one where you can tell the truth without fear of instant punishment or platform loss, your body is allowed to be present (tears, shaking, silence, laughter), the listener is more interested in your heart than your image, and the goal is not to get you back on stage quickly, but to help you return to being a beloved son or daughter.

Three Non-Negotiables to Look For

When you're choosing a Pastoral Partnership space, look for:

1. **Confidentiality with clear boundaries**

   Your story is held with care — and there are clear ethical limits if someone is at risk of harm.

2. **Independence**

   It helps when the person supporting you isn't your direct boss, board member, or someone who controls your role.

3. **Prayerful, trauma-aware presence**

   Not just fixing or advice — but attentiveness to your story, your nervous system, and the gentle leadership of the Holy Spirit.

Questions to Ask Before You Begin

You can ask these directly (and a safe person won't be threatened by them):

- How do you handle confidentiality, and what are the limits?

- Are you independent from my leadership structure or employer?

- What is your training and experience with trauma-aware care?

- What does a typical session look like?

- Do you offer prayer, silence, and space to listen for Jesus, or is it purely conversational?

- How do you support someone carrying temptation, burnout, or conflict without shaming them?

- What would make you recommend counselling/therapy alongside this?

Red Flags (When It's Not Safe)

Be cautious if someone:

- Pressures you, rushes you, or overrides your consent
- Uses spiritual language to control, shame, or silence you
- Offers secrecy without clear ethical boundaries
- Makes your story about them, their ministry, or their opinions
- Treats your pain as a problem to fix rather than a person to honour

If You Love a Leader (How to Be Safe Support)

If you're not in formal leadership but you care about someone who is:

- Pray for their inner life, not just their outcomes
- Ask, "How is your heart?" and stay long enough to hear the answer
- Encourage rest without making them feel guilty for needing it
- Normalise support: "It makes sense to have someone to talk to.

A Note on Pace

This work isn't meant to be rushed. Sometimes one conversation opens a door that needs tenderness and time. Healing is layered. Rest is holy.

ADDITIONAL RESOURCES

Connect with Lawrence Prasad

- **Website:** lawrenceprasad.com
- **Email:** info@lawrenceprasad.com

Lawrence is an inner healing minister, pastoral partner and supervisor, and companion to leaders and the wounded. He offers spiritual direction, ministry training, speaking engagements, and resources for those seeking to encounter the Father's love and experience deep heart transformation. Connect with Lawrence to explore how he can walk alongside you or your community on the journey of healing and restoration.

Ministries & Organisations

Professional Pastoral Partnership (USA - North America)

- **Website:** pastoralpartnership.com
- **Email:** info@pastoralpartnership.com
- **Facebook:** pastoralpartnership
- **Instagram:** @pastoralpartnership

For individuals in the USA and Canada, **Professional Pastoral Partnership** provides independent, confidential pastoral supervision for ministry leaders, pastors, priests, and caregivers. In a safe, non-evaluative space, leaders can process their inner world, explore the hidden pressures of ministry, and receive care for their own hearts. Supervision is not about performance review or accountability — it's about creating a sacred space where those who care for others can be cared for themselves. **Professional Pastoral Partnership** is committed to helping leaders stay healthy, whole, and grounded in their calling.

Restore — A Catch The Fire Ministry

- **Website:** restoremin.au
- **Email:** info@restoremin.au
- **Facebook:** restoremin.au
- **Instagram:** @restoremin.au

For the world to encounter God's transforming presence.

For groups and faith communities worldwide, Restore is a **Catch The Fire** ministry — part of a family of churches and ministries worldwide — birthed from the revival that began in Toronto in 1994. Co-directed by Lawrence Prasad, Restore's desire is to demonstrate our oneness with the Trinity as we share the Father's love, seeing every heart healed, transformed, and restored to the Father's original design.

Heart Keys (Australia & New Zealand)

- **Website:** heartkeys.com.au
- **Email:** info@heartkeys.com.au
- **Instagram:** @heart.keys
- **Facebook:** Heart Keys

For individuals in Australia and New Zealand, **Heart Keys** is a ministry dedicated to inner healing and heart transformation. Through one-on-one prayer ministry, workshops, and training, **Heart Keys** helps individuals encounter the Trinity in their stories, heal from the inside out, and step into their true identity as beloved sons and daughters of the Father. **Heart Keys** offers a safe, trauma-aware, Spirit-led approach to healing that honours each person's journey and invites Jesus into the deepest places of pain, shame, and wounding.

Inner Healing Approaches

Below are a few ministries and approaches that many people have found helpful on the healing journey. Each has its own language, emphasis, and method — so as always, go gently, stay discerning, and choose what feels safe and life-giving for you.

- **HeartSync Healing**

  A biblical inner healing approach that focuses on helping people bring the "parts of the heart" into alignment and connection with God, supporting emotional healing and restored relationship with Him.

  https://heartsynchealing.org

- **Australian Inner Healing Network (AIHN)**

  A national network that champions inner healing ministry in Australia, promoting unity, collaboration, training, and shared standards across a range of Christian inner healing approaches.

  https://www.innerhealing.org.au

- **Elijah House Ministries**

  A Christ-centred ministry dedicated to helping people heal from emotional and spiritual wounds through teaching, prayer ministry, and heart-focused discipleship, with an emphasis on freedom, forgiveness, and wholeness.

https://elijahhouse.org

- **Face to Face Network (Immanuel Approach)**

Helps people connect with Jesus for emotional healing and restoration, using the Immanuel Approach to address trauma, uncover lies, and support lasting transformation through relational connection with God.

https://www.facetofacenetwork.org

- **Bethel Sozo**

Described as a gentle yet powerful tool for inner healing and deliverance, designed to help people deepen their relationship with God by identifying and addressing roots of pain, lies, and patterns that hinder connection.

https://www.bethelsozo.com

- **The Immanuel Approach (Lehman/Wilder)**

A prayer and ministry model for emotional healing and life that aims to deepen intimacy with Jesus, resolve past pain, and discern God's ongoing guidance — integrating relational connection and practical, accessible tools.

https://www.immanuelapproach.com

A Note on Discernment & Professional Support

These resources are offered as options, not prescriptions. Different people find help in different places, and sometimes professional support (GP, psychologist, counsellor, trauma-informed therapist) is also an important part of the journey.

ABOUT THE AUTHOR

Lawrence Prasad is an inner healing minister, pastoral partner and supervisor, and companion to leaders and the wounded — a charismatic revivalist with a contemplative heart. A storyteller by nature, his life has taken him from a childhood steeped in Catholic and charismatic spirituality, through years in Melbourne's gay club and drag scene, to a profound encounter with the Father's outrageous love that changed everything.

Born in Australia to a Catholic family shaped by the Catholic Charismatic Renewal, Lawrence carried both deep spiritual hunger and deep wounding. After years in the club scene, drag performance, and drug world, he experienced a life-changing encounter with the Father at **Catch the Fire's International Leaders School of Ministry** (ILSOM) in 2011. Since then, the Father has gently healed childhood trauma, re-fathered his heart, and led him from shame and striving into beloved sonship.

Out of this journey, Lawrence founded **Heart Keys**, a ministry dedicated to inner healing and heart transformation in Australia, helping people encounter the Trinity in their stories and heal from the inside out. He also leads **Professional Pastoral Partnership** in the USA, providing independent pastoral care and safe, confidential spaces for pastors, priests, and ministry leaders to process their inner world and stay healthy in their calling.

Lawrence is passionate about creating environments where people can be real, vulnerable, and deeply loved, without shame, pretence, or religious performance. His ministry flows from the conviction that one healed heart can change a family, a community, and even a generation.

He lives in Melbourne, Australia, where he continues to write, minister, and walk with others into the Father's outrageous love.

A FINAL BLESSING

As I finish these pages, my prayer for you is simple:

That you would know deep in your bones that you are loved.

That you would awaken and encounter the Father's outrageous love in ways that undo you and remake you.

That you would experience Jesus in your story, not as a distant judge, but as the One who never turned away.

That you would feel the Holy Spirit's comfort, guidance, and gentle conviction leading you into freedom.

I bless your heart to heal.

I bless your memories to be visited by the presence of God.

I bless your identity to be rooted in sonship, not striving.

I bless your relationships to be marked by honesty, grace, and healthy boundaries.

I bless your future to be different from your past, not because you try harder, but because love has done a deeper work.

May you become a living testimony that:

One healed heart can change a family.

One healed heart can change a community.

One healed heart can change a generation.

And may you discover, again and again, that in every chapter of your story:

He never turned away.

Amen.

With much love and blessings,
Lawrence